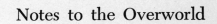

Notes to the Overworld

"There are no dead."
—Maeterlinck, *The Blue Bird*

Notes to
the Overworld

Carroll E. Simcox

THE SEABURY PRESS · NEW YORK

Copyright © 1972 by Carroll E. Simcox
Library of Congress Catalog Card Number: 72-81029
ISBN: 0-8164-0242-6
753-872-C-5
Design by Paula Wiener
Printed in the United States of America

Grateful acknowledgment is made to the following for permission to quote copyrighted material from the authors and titles listed:

Holt, Rinehart, & Winston—Robert Frost, "New Hampshire." Copyright 1923 by Henry Holt & Co.; copyright renewed 1951 by Robert Frost.
Mr. Virgil Markham—Edwin Markham, "The Nail-Torn God."

"However rare true love may be, true friendship is rarer," said La Rochefoucauld. This book is dedicated, *con amore,* to true friends JOHN AND STELLA PIERSON.

Dear Reader:

I could have called these notes *Letters from the Underworld,* but Fyodor Dostoevsky preempted that title many years ago. So *Notes to the Overworld* it is. Some fastidious minds who want Heaven demythologized and despatialized will regret my use of the word "Overworld" because of its primitive cosmological connotations. I want to assure them that the Overworld of my conception is beyond time and space: the Beyond is the Within. The Overworld is not a Beautiful Isle of Somewhere beyond the bright blue sky. It is too real for that—and too close.

Carroll E. Simcox

Notes to

St. John the Elder, 34
Pope John XXIII, 24
Dr. Samuel Johnson, 19, 82, 95
Thomas à Kempis, 73
The Duc de La Rochefoucauld, 45
William Law, 86
C. S. Lewis, 96, 126
Sinclair Lewis, 38
Abraham Lincoln, 54
David Livingstone, 40
James Russell Lowell, 78
Martin Luther, 79
Sir Henry Maine, 104
Malcolm X, 71
Edwin Markham, 117
Karl Marx, 48
Mrs. Karl Marx, 49
Herman Melville, 106
Alfred, Lord Milner, 70
John Milton, 51
William Morris, 84
Reinhold Niebuhr, 59, 110
Blaise Pascal, 12
St. Paul the Apostle, 75
Wendell Phillips, 115

Alexander Pope, 42
Ernest Renan, 31
Will Rogers, 35
Romain Rolland, 55
Richard Rolle of Hampole, 13
Bertrand Russell, 109
Moshe Leib Sassover, 68
George Bernard Shaw, 10
Carroll E. Simcox, 28
King Solomon, 66
Herbert Spencer, 60
Baruch Spinoza, 105
Adlai E. Stevenson, 29
Robert Louis Stevenson, 9
Jonathan Swift, 97
Cornelius Tacitus, 14
Pierre Teilhard de Chardin, S.J., 116
William Temple, 100
James Thurber, 17
Anthony Trollope, 25
Jean Vianney, the Curé d'Ars, 74
George Washington, 122
Alfred North Whitehead, 102
Oscar Wilde, 18, 112
Roger Williams, 94

To Robert Louis Stevenson:

It is reported that when you heard of Matthew Arnold's death you remarked: "Poor Arnold—he's dead now—gone to Heaven; and he won't like God." Is he still maladjusted? I imagine you're happy because very busy; it was said that you died with a thousand untold stories in your heart. A pity you can't get them published down here; we need very badly some good stories of the sort you told, some good jokes, some good new songs. But the primary purpose of this note is to suggest that you drop in at poor Arnold's mansion and see if he is at least reconciled if not blissful. If he's lusting for the fleshpots of earth tell him from me that things here have gone from bad to worse. Philistinism is rampant everywhere. There are worse places than Heaven. That should give him a lift.

To George Bernard Shaw:

I learned this morning of the death of a friend who in his virtues was Christ-like and in his weaknesses pathetic. He was killed in an auto accident. His wife called me, and though she loved him dearly she said: "Somehow I feel it was a promotion for him." However that may be, I've been thinking about one of your *Maxims for Revolutionaries*: "Life levels all men; death reveals the eminent." Life not only "leveled" my friend, it laid him flat for much of his time. And now that he's dead, he's not going to be "eminent" in the world's sense of the term, but that isn't what you meant anyway. By dying he has taken on a strange eminence in my heart. Like Rip Van Winkle, he was always much more useful to others than to himself. This is one of the apostolic virtues St. Paul speaks of in II Corinthians 6: "As poor, yet making many rich."

I am comforted by your reminder of how life levels and death reveals. Life no longer flattens my friend. Death reveals him for what he is—a prince fallen in Israel.

To Dante Alighieri:

Your poetry stands up wonderfully after six centuries. Your vision of *L'amor che muove il sole e l'altre stelle*—"The love that moves the sun and the other stars"—has been the vision of God by which all earnest Christians have walked from the beginning until now. I'm sorry to report that many of today's theologians simply ignore the created universe as a panorama of God's love and identify God's love exclusively with man's love for his neighbor. When *you* read St. John's words —"God is love"—you understood him. These modern theologians do not (or they disagree with him). They believe rather that "love is God." They think this is bringing God down to earth, humanizing him. Surely it is not God who needs to be humanized; it's man.

And how about this? When the modern theologian wants to reject and condemn some part of the Christian faith which he doesn't believe, he calls it "medieval." *That* for you —and Thomas Aquinas—and Francis of Assisi!

To Blaise Pascal:

I've been thinking about this one of your *Pensées*: "The infinite distance between body and mind is a symbol of the infinitely more infinite distance between mind and charity; for charity is supernatural." As I read you, charity isn't just an expression or refinement of mind, so that the more intelligent one is the more charitable he must be; charity is categorically other than mind. Man is born with mind and can naturally achieve mental growth and fulfilment. Charity is supernatural; one can only receive it as a special gift (*donum superadditum*) from God, and can grow in it only by prayer and fasting, and hard effort animated by grace. Dietrich Bonhoeffer warned us against "cheap grace." I take your statement as an implicit and much needed warning against "cheap charity." We contemporary Americans, at any rate, find it easy to say of somebody, or to imagine of our own dear selves: "He's just a natural 'lovin' sort of a guy' —everybody's friend—not a mean streak in him." Bosh! You knew better. We all should, and we all would if it were not for this damned egotistical habit of crediting ourselves with a superabundance of supernatural charity. Thomas Hood wasn't a great poet, but he saw the plain truth of this matter when he lamented—

> Alas! for the rarity
> Of Christian charity
> Under the sun!

Charity, like grace, is free for the asking from God. But it is never cheap, never easy, and never common.

To Richard Rolle of Hampole:

I've just written a note to your contemporary Dante, whose companionship I imagine you are enjoying. I was deploring to him the way in which modernest theologians try to comprehend the love of God within the cramped and leaky confines of a man's love for his neighbor. Your line came to mind: "Luf copuls god & manne." We have improved on your spelling (or think we have), but not on your theology. If you haven't yet met your English countryman, the poet Coleridge, seek him out and ask him to recite for you his *Rime of the Ancient Mariner.* You'll love it and you may be thrilled to tears by the portion of the "rime" in which the mariner in his desperate plight watched the watersnakes:

> O happy living things! no tongue
> Their beauty might declare:
> A spring of love gush'd from my heart,
> And I bless'd them unaware:
> Sure my kind saint took pity on me,
> And I bless'd them unaware.
>
> The selfsame moment I could pray;
> And from my neck so free
> The Albatross fell off, and sank
> Like lead into the sea.

You and Coleridge should be wonderfully congenial. I trust that you, a former resident of what used to be called Merrie England, find your present abode even merrier.

To Cornelius Tacitus:

I am astonished that so few moralists ponder this truth which you stated so succinctly: "It is human nature to hate the man you have hurt" (*Proprium humani ingenii est odisse quem laeseris*. Agricola 42). Jews and Christians have an eloquent example in their holy scriptures. Amnon, son of King David, seduced his beautiful half-sister, Tamar. "Then Amnon hated her exceedingly; so that the hatred wherewith he hated her was greater than the love wherewith he had loved her" (II Samuel 13:15). We citizens of the great American republic have as much "human nature" as other people. Earlier in our history while we were taking over this land from the Indians, largely by force and fraud, we adopted the comforting maxim that "the only good Indian is a dead Indian." It made it easier to live with ourselves if we could hate the victim of our rapacity. Many American whites have hated blacks for the same reason. To hate the man one has hurt is "human nature"—and we all seem to have it. Earlier in your century, a then obscure Palestinian Jew thought it was about time we did something about our "human nature." He suggested repenting it. It's still about time.

To Bishop Charles Gore:

I've just come back from a visit to our Milwaukee zoo, which is one of the finest. A remark about zoos which you once made to William Temple is bugging me. Temple was taking some children to a zoo when he met you. When he told you where they were going, you said: "Oh, I do hate the zoo. It makes me an atheist in twenty minutes." You, of all people! How any man can watch monkeys playing and have doubts about God is beyond me. My troubles with theistic belief begin not at the zoo, to which I go to recharge my faith, but when I read the newspaper, or when I listen to human beings made in the divine image talking about each other behind their backs.

I hope you didn't really mean it. Recall that passage in Sir Thomas Browne's *Religio Medici*: "I hold there is a general beauty in the works of God, and therefore no deformity in any kind or species of creature whatsoever. I cannot tell by what Logick we call a Toad, a Bear, or an Elephant ugly; they being created in those outward shapes and figures which best express the actions of their inward forms, and having past that general Visitation of God, Who saw that all that He had made was good, that is, comfortable to His Will, which abhors deformity, and is the rule of order and beauty."

Better yet, talk it over with Sir Thomas in person. Then try the zoo again.

To Jesus ben Sirach:

I marvel at how seldom Ecclesiasticus is quoted by people who relish a happy union of style with substance. It must be that too few read it. If I were a professor of political science, I would have my students memorize this golden text: "As is the lust of an eunuch to deflower a virgin, so he is that executeth judgment with violence" (Ecclesiasticus 20:4). Something along this line that Talleyrand once said to Napoleon is often quoted: "You can do everything with bayonets, Sire, except sit on them!" He put it well; you put it better, because more subtly. Commonly it is true that the unjust man can be restrained only by force; but the restraint of injustice is one thing, the establishment of justice quite another. The man afire with zeal for justice who tries to execute it by violence is as pitiably frustrate as the lustful eunuch. Justice is established only when all parties eagerly embrace it with free wills and resolutely purpose to fulfill it. The righteous hothead with an itch for justice in his head and a club in his hand is wont to bellow, "By God, if they don't want justice I'll pound it into them!" The job of the wise is to make this fool realize his tactical impotence.

I would have my students read you and Machiavelli. Note the order.

16

To James Thurber:

I learned only today that you died a very disappointed man —that you had longed in vain for a Nobel prize. "You'd think that they might give it to a humorist once," you complained. I don't blame you. You were more than right. When shall we learn that he who brings laughter to the soul not only entertains us but edifies us—builds us up in life? A recent experience corroborates my, and your, conviction about the tonic power of humor. A friend of mine has been wretchedly sick for many months, with one of those ailments that defy diagnosis and sure-fire treatment. Old Doc Simcox (that's me) thought that with all the other medicinal things she is taking, a spot of P. G. Wodehouse wouldn't do her any harm, so I sent her a copy of *Leave It to Psmith*. It worked splendidly. Sure, we're praying for her, too. But I think God slipped that prescription into my mind. After all, King Solomon was hardly a dope, and you remember what he said: "A merry heart doeth good like a medicine" (Proverbs 17:22).

To Oscar Wilde:

"There is no sin except stupidity," you said. This remark does credit to neither your heart nor your head, nor even your wit. You could say it blithely because, whatever else you were, you were obviously not stupid. So, pronouncing that there is no sin except stupidity, you give yourself a total absolution and a perfectly clean bill of health. I am sure you now regret having said it. It is not very clever, and it is very false. Honest and invincible stupidity in anybody is a worse affliction than any other handicap; but to call it a sin is outrageous. *Pride* is the root sin. You yourself said this, in a hundred different ways. I have never known a stupid person who was proud of his stupidity. I have known some stupid people who were proud of what they, poor dunces, fondly thought was their cleverness, but their sin was in their pride, not in their stupidity.

This hasn't been a very pleasant note, and next time I'll try to be more agreeable. I am one of your fans. But, as you know, nothing makes us hotter under the collar than a lapse by our lion.

To Dr. Samuel Johnson:

After Boswell had told you all you needed to hear about a fallen lady, attempting, as he himself put it, to palliate what he was sensible could not be justified, you pronounced: "My dear Sir, never accustom your mind to mingle virtue and vice. The woman's a whore, and there's an end on't." This seems rather harsh, albeit true. A whore is a whore is a whore, but surely there are differing reasons for becoming whores and differing degrees of culpability in any transgression. But I take it that what taxed your patience was the gallant Boswell's implicit intent to call a whore by some other name. The Boswells are still with us. They teach us that a drunkard is an alcoholic, a rich thief is a kleptomaniac (as Ambrose Bierce pointed out in his *Devil's Dictionary*), a sluggard in school is an underachiever, etc., etc. And oh yes: The U.S. Army's new training manual has changed the words to be used in bayonet drill. The trainees formerly shouted "Kill! Kill!" as they rammed their bayonets into dummies. Now they are to shout "Yah! Yah!" But don't ask me why. *You* are the lexicographer.

To Albert Camus:

I want to tell you how much I appreciate your noble aphorism, "To grow old is to pass from passion to compassion." You realize, of course, that this doesn't always happen; it's what always ought to happen. This is the kind of maxim which, when it captures the mind, helps to bring itself to pass in the life. In our contemporary American culture we badly need a positive lore of growing old. Americans are not supposed to grow old—it's against the mores. I'd like to propose to the United States Congress that on all our national currency, for one year's time, might be inscribed the counsel of Theopompos of Chios (4th cent., B.C.): "An unseemly fascination with youth is the surest sign of old age." But I would be dismissed as some kind of a nut, so I'll just grump about it to you. I submit that in a healthy culture all people grow old in the joyous spirit of Browning's Rabbi ben Ezra, knowing that "the best is yet to be—the last of life, for which the first was made." Somebody should write a thoroughly Christian book on growing old. But it could get him into trouble with the cultural vigilantes who regard growing old as a subversive activity.

To Thomas Carlyle:

"If Jesus Christ were to come today, people would not even crucify him," you mused. "They would ask him to dinner, and hear what he had to say, and make fun of it." I wonder. The question is often discussed today. Should we psychoanalyze him, pop him into jail, or what? Perhaps some would be amused by him, but I find this the least plausible possibility. I think the dominant reactions to him would be hatred, adoration, and bewilderment; I won't guess in what order. This is how it was at his First Coming; there is no hint in the Gospels that anybody made fun of him. You knew your Victorian contemporaries as I do not, but I doubt that the reaction to Jesus in any age would be much different from what it was in first-century Palestine. I suspect that William Hazlitt comes closest to the truth in his famous passage in the essay *Of Persons One Would Wish to Have Seen*:

" 'There is only one person I can ever think of after this,' continued H—; but without mentioning a name that once put on a semblance of mortality. 'If Shakespeare was to come into the room, we should all rise up to meet him; but if that person was to come into it, we should all fall down and try to kiss the hem of his garment!'

"As a lady present seemed now to get uneasy at the turn the conversation had taken, we rose up to go."

To Oliver Wendell Holmes, Jr.:

Today I came upon one of your strong and splendid dicta. I wish I had had it to quote many times in the recent past as I have listened to some of my contemporaries extolling "the sacredness of human life" while denigrating "law and order." You said: "The sacredness of human life is a formula that is good only inside a system of law." I should think we could quote that and say "Nuff said," and consider the subject closed; but it doesn't always work in that nice reasonable way nowadays. We have "gut-thinking" now, and this, as you have already guessed, is thinking that is not done with the mind. It's something like playing the piano with the toes.

To Master Aristotle:

I am a Committee of One, deriving my authority from the consent of the Committee, to tell the world about one thing you wrote in the *Nichomachean Ethics*: "The doctor's business is not to take our health into his keeping but to give it a chance." Evidently you saw many a patient medicated to death. This has been going on right down to now. There are a hundred variations on the old sick joke about how the operation was successful but the patient died, and the joke is at the expense of the doctors. But the fault or failure is surely not all theirs. When we go to the doctor we want him to take our health into his keeping and establish it with the wave of a pill. People get not only the rulers they want but the doctors they want. The healer who strives to get us to take proper care of ourselves and thus to give our health a chance has a hard time with us. We prefer the quack who promises what we want—purchasable health. If people can be persuaded to believe what you said, we shall all be better off, doctors and patients both.

To Pope John XXIII:

As you must know by now, you did many wonderful things for countless people. I want to tell you what you did for me: You were a living answer to my question, What does a Christian look like? Cardinal Suenens noted that you were astonishingly natural in the supernatural and supernatural in the natural. You were natural, at ease, at home, with God; but when you went down to visit the prisons in Rome, you saw and embraced God in those human riff-raff. In all of your being this way, natural with God and supernatural with people, you showed me what a Christian looks like.

I edit an Anglican weekly magazine called *The Living Church*. One of our poets, Robert Hale, wrote for us a verse which expresses this mystery of Christian being which glowed through you. It runs:

> The best things I have done for Christ
>   were carrying books for a boy on crutches,
>   reading to a blind student,
>   and letting my folks
>   have the car on their anniversary.
> The best things I have done for others
>   were going on a retreat,
>   climbing the hill to the cross,
>   and praying—alone.[1]

I thought you'd like this. It says what you said, what you were.

[1] For author's references, see page 127.

To Anthony Trollope:

One of several things that make your novels a delight is your open, shameless moralizing along the way. I like such writing, especially when the author is as good a novelist and as good a moralist as you. But at one point you nod, as a moralist; *bonus dormitat Homerus.* It's in the second chapter of *Barchester Towers,* in the midst of your soliloquy upon how much kinder is God to us than we to ourselves, how "at the last going of every well-beloved one, we all doom ourselves to an eternity of sorrow" but the sorrow lasts for but a very short time—thanks to God. All very sound and true, except for this one shocking statement: " 'Let me ever remember my living friends, but forget them as soon as dead,' was the prayer of a wise man who understood the mercy of God." I cannot agree. I think the contrary is true. It is by the mercy of God that we *remember,* not *forget,* our departed friends —not in eternal sorrow but in love, gratitude, and intimate communion with them. Why should we try or want to forget them? By the mercy of God there is everything to gain by remembering. They live. They love us. They want our continuing love. I am as sure of this as I am sure that you are reading this note at this moment; and I am almost as sure that you are genially recognizing that my point is well taken. We believe in the communion of saints.

To Democritus of Abdera:

The fragments of your wisdom which have come down to us from pre-Socratic Greek antiquity are, in the words of Tennyson about the Duke of Wellington, "rich in saving common-sense." Common-sense is a quality which almost everybody blandly assumes he has by the barrel load and which is in fact as rare as beauty or intelligence. Unless some angel was your ghost-writer you had it, in evidence whereof I quote this saying of yours: "In old age, a man is agreeable if his manner is pleasant and his speech serious." Too many old men (and old women) make the mistake of being cute—"seventy-five years young!" Younger folk always hope that the old man will be pleasant, but they expect him to be serious if he has enough intelligence to be worth knowing. You are entirely right. On this subject, George Santayana said something that should be kept at hand for constant ready reference: "The young man who has not wept is a savage; the old man who will not laugh is a fool." The two of you, in these two sentences, have taught us much of the art of being worthy of the gift and privilege of old age.

To Nathan Hale:

Somebody recently made a survey of history books used in our public schools. Included were fourteen books written several decades ago and forty-five more recent ones which are still in use. In eleven of the older ones, readers are told of your last words: "I only regret that I have but one life to lose for my country." In only one of the forty-five newer ones is this mentioned. I want to apologize to you for this national disgrace. These newer books were written by people who call themselves "liberals." The label seems grotesque when applied to people who seem ashamed to belong to a nation "conceived in liberty." An English war nurse, Edith Cavell, was put to death by the Germans in 1915. She said before she died: "I realize that patriotism is not enough. I must have no hatred or bitterness towards anyone." She is commonly quoted, and you are not. Those who quote her but not you imagine that she was above patriotism and that you were not. They are wrong about both of you. She, like you, died for a free nation, not for "one world." You, like her, had no hatred or bitterness toward anyone. A free world community can be built only by free peoples. You and Miss Cavell saw that; today's liberal doctorers of history do not.

A modern Englishman well said that patriotism makes a man a gentleman, but nationalism makes him a cad. You, sir, were a great gentleman, and despite the efforts of the anti-patriots you are not forgotten.

Overworld
Oct. 5, 1971 (Earth time)

To Carroll E. Simcox:

Nathan Hale is playing golf with John André, for whom he feels a special kinship, so he has asked me to reply to your noble effort to rehabilitate him in men's eyes—though he feels no particular need for rehabilitation, and has long since ceased to regret that he has not another earthly life to live. (Some of us who have tried reincarnation have died to regret the experiment.) Edith Cavell, whom I saw at lunch with Florence Nightingale, also thanks you for your kind words about her.

As my contribution to the subject, I would ask: What do we mean by patriotism in the context of our times? (Pardon me, *your* times.) It seems to me that a patriotism that puts country ahead of self is what counts; a patriotism which is not short, frenzied outbursts of emotion, but the tranquil and steady dedication of a lifetime. There are words that are easy to utter, but this is a mighty assignment. For it is often easier to fight for principles than to live up to them.

When an American says that he loves his country, he means not only that he loves the New England hills, the prairies gleaming in the sun, the great mountains, the wide and rising plains, and the sea. He means that he loves an inner air, an inner light in which freedom lives and in which a man can draw the breath of self-respect.

I have an idea that I said much the same thing while I was with you on earth. Yes, on reference to Bartlett, I find that it was in a speech in New York City on August 27, 1952; I didn't think anyone was listening at the time. Whatever became of New York, by the way? People arriving from there of late seem so bruised and battered that they don't want to talk about it.

Oh, oh, I'd better stop. Here comes Samuel Johnson, and you know what *he* thought about patriotism!

> *Faithfully yours,*
> *Adlai E. Stevenson*

To Adlai E. Stevenson:

I welcome you to my host of wise and witty pen pals.

Since you ask what we mean by patriotism in the context of our times, and then go on to tell me what you think we ought to mean, I reply simply that I think your answer superb in every way and accept it as my own. On the day of Queen Victoria's burial, Gilbert Chesterton wrote: "It is sometimes easy to give one's country blood and easier to give her money. Sometimes the hardest thing is to give her truth." Only a great patriot understands that. Chesterton was such. So were you.

And at the risk of disagreeing with you, I submit that so was Samuel Johnson. I imagine that in your reference to "what *he* thought of patriotism" you have in mind his saying that "patriotism is the last refuge of the scoundrel" and I think that you misunderstand him. As I read him, trying to see him steadily and see him whole, his patriotism was so ardent that he couldn't endure the spectacle of scoundrels taking refuge in it. We get a much more direct and eloquent expression of Johnson's mind about patriotism in this sentence: "That man is little to be envied whose patriotism would not gain force upon the plain of Marathon, or whose piety would not grow warmer among the ruins of Iona." By the way, do they speak better English than that even in Overworld?

As for what's becoming of New York, perhaps what the city needs is a good law-and-order Democrat for mayor. I would suggest your own Dick Daley, but that would probably mean losing the Episcopal Church Center to some other place.

Affectionately,
Carroll E. Simcox

P.S. I remember that you were not an Episcopalian, so the last sentence above may puzzle you. After the civil disorder in Mayor Daley's Chicago at the time of the 1968 Democratic National Convention, the Episcopal Church's Executive Council severely punished His Honor by declaring a one-year boycott of Chicago as a place where Executive Council-related meetings might be held. The Daley machine staggered through this somehow.

To Ernest Renan:

You were usually a master of Gallic clarity, but your comment on the Book of Ecclesiastes baffles me. You said that it was the only pleasant book ever written by a Jew. Your statement contains two assertions, both of which I think are false: that Ecclesiastes is a pleasant book, and that no other Jew ever wrote pleasantly. What about your contemporary Heinrich Heine? Despite his formal conversion to Christianity, he was esthetically, emotionally, a Hebrew of the Hebrews. He delighted in such pleasantries as "God will forgive me—that's his specialty!" That this is also an inanity is not to my present point. Recently I've been reading an anthology of Yiddish stories, some of which date from long before your time. In them is much that is pleasant, amusing, even hilarious. So much for your assertion about Jewish literature in general.

Ecclesiastes is indeed beautiful writing, but just about the last adjective that would come to my mind to describe it is "pleasant." It is drenched with the Tears of Things. Its writer denounces laughter as "mad." His verdict on this world and all that therein is could be summed up in the words of Queen Victoria when somebody tried to entertain her and flunked: "We are not amused!" A man not amused himself has no desire to be amusing; and this man wasn't, and hadn't.

To William Blake:

Do you remember the moment you tell about in *The Marriage of Heaven and Hell*: you were sitting on a pleasant river bank by moonlight, and you heard a harper singing? "The man who never alters his opinion is like standing water, & breeds reptiles of the mind." For me this is not a comfortable word. I pride myself upon the firmness and fixedness of my opinions. When the other fellow is this way, it's because he's pigheaded; when I'm this way it's because I'm strong and stable—Old Hickory standing at Armageddon to fight the battle of the Lord. You assume that your harper came from Above rather than Below. St. John wisely counsels us to try the spirits to see whether they be of God. I'm afraid there can be no doubt about this one. His song is a true word of the Lord to us all. I do not warmly welcome it, but I'm sure I need it.

William E. Gladstone speaks of an important distinction we must make: "Many men know their opinions, few their convictions; but in the long run convictions rule, opinions go to the wall." I can only hope that what I think are my convictions are not just stupid and sterile opinions aswarm with reptiles of the mind. Your harper friend's word reminds me of another one that shakes me whenever it gets past my mental censor to the interior: "When that man is thinking, he is simply rearranging his prejudices." I often wonder if other people have as much trouble keeping their opinions reasonably fluid as I have.

To Charles Robert Darwin:

You had to endure in your lifetime, and since, an unconscionable amount of senseless ridicule from Christian people who failed to understand your ideas and failed also to appreciate your spirit of humble and courageous truthfulness. In your *Descent of Man* (why didn't you call it *Ascent of Man?*) you said: "We must acknowledge, it seems to me, that man with all his noble qualities still bears in his bodily frame the indelible stamp of his lowly origin." There seems to me nothing shameful about coming from a lowly origin, and I am astounded by the snappishness of Christians—of all people!—who detest the thought of it. One would think it all the better cause to glorify the God who "raiseth up the poor out of the dust, and lifteth the needy out of the dunghill" (Psalm 113:7). The things we have to be ashamed of do not pertain to our "bodily frame" at all, but to our self-chosen spiritual frame. As physical creatures of God's love we emerged from the primordial slime because he raised us from it. We have created a spiritual slime of our own in which to wallow. *This* is the infamy.

To St. John the Elder:

I get my idea of ideal Christianity largely from you, but one statement of yours puzzles me. No, that isn't it; I understand it but I disagree. It's this: "The man who says 'I love God' but hates his brother lies; for if he does not love his brother, whom he has seen, how can he love God, whom he has not seen?" (I John 4:20.) We have no argument about this man's mendacity, but I wish you had not suggested the very dubitable proposition that seeing a man makes it easier to love him. Doesn't that depend on which brother we are talking about? Very often we must love a man in spite of seeing him, not because of it, for the reason that there's something in him that we abhor. Many years ago I got into correspondence with a man living in St. Paul. Never have I plunged into a delightful friendship more quickly. Our communion by mail was pure joy. One day I found that I was soon to be in St. Paul, and I told him the good news that we should be meeting in the flesh. He replied by special delivery: "Don't. Our friendship is too good to risk spoiling. We might both be disappointed." Being very young and inexperienced, I thought his reasoning quite wacky. In the ensuing forty years of trying to love my unseen God and my seen neighbor, I have grown to appreciate my friend's realistic sanity. If he's right about this, you have to be wrong. I wish the critics would discover that I St. John 4:20b is a Gnostic interpolation. Maybe they will.

To Will Rogers:

You were past 50 when you said that you had never met a man you didn't like. We know that you meant it, and we can only ponder your achievement (for that's what it was) with awe and envy. You had a peerless gift for friendship. What I'd like to know now is what you would say if you had met some of the world's nastiest people, and it occurs to me that, under the conditions of eternity, perhaps you have. My question: How do you like Adolf Hitler? Nabal the Carmelite (that fellow in I Samuel 25)? Or this one—the man who poisoned my dog, nearly 50 years ago? In my intercessory prayers I sometimes try to recall all who have ever hurt me and have now left this life. I ask for them God's pardon and peace, and the light of the Everlasting Mercy. I include this man. It's the best I can do for him—to pray that he has changed. But if you have met him, and he has not changed, did you like him? What is it to like somebody? Isn't it to be attracted to him, to enjoy his company, to give him Brownie points, to approve of him? I find it incredible that you, of all people, would like an unrepentant dog poisoner. If ever I learn that you do, I shall be very disappointed in you. The man is entitled to our love and our prayers, but surely not to our liking.

To John Dewey:

Bless you for this just and true word of yours: "The Puritan is never popular, not even in a society of Puritans. In case of a pinch, the mass prefer to be good fellows rather than to be good men." [2] The great truth is that the authentic Puritan really is a good man, not a sanctimonious Pecksniff. His goodness shows up the rest of us. "He hath a daily beauty in his life which makes us ugly." In our day when a person says, "Of course I'm no Puritan!" what he's really claiming is that he's one of his Maker's masterpieces, for he has convinced himself that his moral better, the Puritan, is not at all what he seems to be. We slander the Puritan to simplify our own self-apotheosis.

You evidently believed that if we are to give the Devil his due, we should do no less for the man who is better than we are. This is the gallantry of plain decency.

Give my very deep respects to Jonathan Edwards, John Milton, John Bunyan, and all the good Puritans who walk the streets of Heaven. I'm sure they have lost none of their splendid virtues, and I hope they have acquired the virtue of joy and gladness. (Though I'm not forgetting that many of them had it here, in this world, where there wasn't and still isn't nearly so much for godly souls to laugh about.)

To Jacob the Patriarch:

According to the traditional etymology, your name means "one that takes by the heel or supplants; the heeler." Pardon the pun and the resort to modern slang, but in some episodes—for example, your swindling of your brother, Esau, out of his birthright—you were a first-class heel. However, you knew it, and you knew that God knew it; and from this penitent self-knowledge you went on to greatness. I revere you for the usual and proper reasons, but I hope you do not take offense from the fact that always my first thought of you is of your lovely romanticism, superbly told in this verse: "And Jacob served seven years for Rachel; and they seemed unto him but a few days, for the love he had to her" (Genesis 29:20). Reading between the lines, I surmise that this great woman made a complete man out of you. (If I am wrong, don't correct me when we meet. If this is an illusion, I don't want to be disillusioned.) How light and how short is any labor when it is simply a labor of love! Your greatest descendant calls us to love as he loves: he calls it his "yoke" and he tells us that his yoke is easy and his burden is light (Matthew 11:30). He calls us to love God and our neighbor as you loved Rachel. That's asking a lot; but he asks the impossible of us and then enables us to do it. I think that he—humanly your descendant—had something to do with bringing you and Rachel together, and with everything that made you the man you were in the end. "Without him was not anything made that was made" (John 1:3).

To Sinclair Lewis:

Undoubtedly some people were surprised when you said that the author who had influenced you most in your childhood was Sir Thomas Malory. Reportedly you went on to explain: "As a kid my favorite reading was Howard Pyle's King Arthur stories, based on Malory. Well, when I grew up—I found there were no knights in Minnesota." As an admirer of yours, also a fellow Midwesterner and small-town boy and lover of knighthood, I can sympathize with and understand the unhappiness of your disenchantment. But it seems a thousand pities that Mark Twain didn't stand *in loco* Malory in your childhood. In that case I think you might have discovered that although there are no knights in Minnesota, there are people as exciting and admirable and even heroic as any of Malory's figments. We had them over in North Dakota, and I didn't appreciate them at all at the time. A Twain, or a Lewis, could have made immortals out of some of those characters in Park River. Only in the retrospect of forty years am I beginning to see their literary possibilities. Alas, I'm no novelist. Even as a boy, you really should have known better than to look for *knights* in Minnesota. Perhaps this is the supremely serious gravamen against literary romanticism: It makes us look around us today for people who nonexisted a thousand years ago.

To Richard Hooker:

I respectfully suggest that you erred when you wrote: "The general and perpetual voice of men is as the sentence of God himself. For that which all men have at all times learned, Nature herself must needs have taught; and God being the author of Nature, her voice is but his instrument." Your rule cannot be a universal one for it does not cover all cases. I could give you a hundred exceptions to it. One should suffice: the "general and perpetual voice of men" that a rock is made of very solid stuff. We know today that it is made up of charges of energy, not solid in themselves at all. Bishop Berkeley taught that matter as we commonly conceive of it is nonexistent. Samuel Johnson, who should have known better, kicked a large stone and as his foot bounced back declared that he had refuted Berkeley. The "general and perpetual voice of men," what theologians have called "universal consent," would back up Johnson against Berkeley; but Berkeley's strange idea was closer to our twentieth-century scientific understanding of "matter" than was Johnson's. "Universal consent" is not "the sentence of God himself" but simply the state of man's ignorance at the moment.

I agree that, since God is the author of Nature, to tune in on Nature is to tune in on God; but whenever we do so, we learn something we didn't know before. This means that God is leading us into all truth, as he promised. It means also, however, that there is never at any time, on any subject, a "general and perpetual voice of men."

To David Livingstone:

May I presume? You once said something, and I don't know in what context or situation, which has become a proverb. I'm sorry that it has, because as usually quoted and understood it makes you ridiculous and nobody deserves this fate less than you. You said: "Anywhere, provided it be forward." Anybody who will take the trouble to look at your great life will instantly see what you meant. "Forward" meant, for you, in the direction of God, in the steps of Christ, under the guidance of the Holy Spirit; and for you the "anywhere" meant the place where God wanted you to go. But today the statement "Anywhere, provided it be forward!" means simply "Keep moving; any change must be for the better!" A church signboard bore it recently as an inspirational message to passers-by:

ANYWHERE, PROVIDED IT BE FORWARD!
—David Livingstone

Along came a graffitist and inscribed thereunder:

AND SO SAY ALL OF US!
—The Gadarene Swine

I presume that you would agree with him.

To Elizabeth Barrett Browning:

Your husband I find the most inviting and hospitable of the great English poets. You I find almost without peer in the quality of compassion; Blake comes to mind as your great peer in this respect. Beautifully typical are your lines written at Cowper's grave:

> O poets, from a maniac's tongue was poured the
>   deathless singing!
> O Christians, at your cross of hope, a hopeless hand
>   was clinging!
> O men, this man in brotherhood your weary paths
>   beguiling,
> Groaned inly while he taught you peace, and died
>   while ye were smiling.

Chesterton felt that Cowper was driven mad by the pitiless logic of Calvin's doctrine of Predestination, and remarked that the poor man was damned by John Calvin and was almost saved by John Gilpin. That, too, was a thought worthy of a Christian as well as a wit. It probably was the doctrine of Predestination that unhinged Cowper's mind, but regardless of that I think we need to note the paradoxical and inexplicable truth that sometimes we can learn hope from a hopeless teacher and peace from one who is in torment. Only God knows how or why. You wisely refrained from analyzing it in the strange case of Cowper; you simply noted it and bade us feel this example of the Tears of Things.

To Alexander Pope:

The word "obscenity" in current American idiom has become little more than a synonym for "whatever it is that I'm against." It is not limited to the lewd and lascivious but is extended to such things as capitalism when it's a socialist speaking, pacifism when it's a militarist speaking, war when it's a pacifist speaking, chastity when it's a sexologist of the *Playboy* school speaking. But what moves me to write this note is your comment in your "Essay on Criticism":

> No pardon vile Obscenity should find,
> Tho' wit and art conspire to move your mind;
> But Dulness with Obscenity must prove
> As shameful sure as Impotence in love.

Obscenity in art or in life often becomes a bore in an unbelievable hurry; it becomes dullness itself. No wonder you couldn't think of the one without the other.

This will amuse you. One of our great comic actors, the now venerable Groucho Marx, went to see *Hair*, a play in which there is much on-stage nudity. He reported later that having seen the show he went home, took off all his clothes, gazed at himself in the mirror and decided that the show just wasn't worth $11.00.

To St. Gregory of Nyssa:

Reading your splendid sermons on the Lord's Prayer I am amazed at how clearly you speak to me over the gulf of sixteen centuries. But upon one aspect of prayer you seem to me to fall into what the Germans would call an *alttestamentlich* ("Old Testamently") concept. It's in the passage that begins: "If work is preceded by prayer, sin will find no entrance into the soul." Then you say that prayer will not only keep the farmer from sin but that "his fruit will multiply even on a small plot of land." You assure us that "through prayer we obtain physical well-being, a happy home, and a strong, well-ordered society. Prayer will make our nation powerful, will give us victory in war and security in peace. . . . It obtains a good harvest for the farmer and a safe port for the sailor." Does it—always? Our Lord Jesus prayed that the terrible cup might pass from him, but it did not. Shall we say that prayer failed him, or that he failed in prayer? In the same sermon you said: "The effect of prayer is union with God, and if someone is with God he is separated from the enemy." This, now, is Christian talk. William Temple, late Archbishop of Canterbury, said: "The primary and fundamental matter in every real prayer is that a human soul is once again, or for the first time, holding intercourse with its Father." I hope that *this* is the understanding of what we may expect from prayer that your original hearers and your host of readers through the ages have got from you. Any other understanding may be *alttestamentlich* but is surely less than Christian.

To Albert Einstein:

You didn't pretend to be a theologian; indeed, you didn't pretend to be anything. But no Doctor of the Church from St. Paul through Karl Barth ever said it better than you when you said: "God is subtle but he is not malicious." You once explained it with this less felicitous paraphrase: "Nature conceals her mystery by means of her essential grandeur, not by her cunning." My Christian orthodoxy cannot accept your equation of God with Nature. But a wise teacher of my youth taught me that when any man of great wisdom and goodness, like you, says anything whatever, about anything whatsoever, I must sift the words for that jewel of truth which is most indubitably there. Your statement about God's unmalicious subtlety confirms my faith that I don't have to understand God in order to trust with complete confidence that what he is doing is better than anything I can desire or pray for.

Your countryman Gerhard Tersteegen said that a comprehended God would be no God at all. He was a Christian pietist, you a Jewish rationalist; but to me you say what he said—at least as well if not better. *Dankeschön!*

To the Duc de La Rochefoucauld:

I love your maxims. One of them comes especially to mind as I think about what we call nowadays situation ethics: "If you think you love your mistress for her own sake, you are quite mistaken." One of the postulates of the situationists is that it is possible for two people to love one another quite purely, each for the sake of the other, and that if they do so love one another there's no good reason why they shouldn't go to bed together. Poor St. Augustine is brutally misquoted in support of a moral principle he would reject with horror. He is quoted as saying, "Love and do as you please." What he clearly meant is that if you love God and your neighbor as you ought, your conduct will take care of itself.

Long before modern situation ethics was dreamt of, people who wanted to fornicate felt the need to convince themselves that it wasn't just fornication, or really fornication, at all; said the man: "I love this beautiful daughter of God for her own dear sake. This being so, I owe it to both of us to commit what those loveless and hypocritical moralists nastily call 'fornication' but which is in fact loving her for her own sake."

You knew better. It's a pity everybody doesn't. The primrose path is heavily infested with such poison ivy.

To Mohandas Gandhi:

You were one of the supremely wise, good, and great men of our age despite your hatred of the human body, which you called "a filthy mass of bones, flesh and blood, exuding breath and water that are full of poison." As a Christian I believe that God creates this body, so it must be good in itself. The Son of God took the body of flesh upon himself and showed us its glory as an instrument of holy living. To be sure, there are evil and destructive passions in every human life that need to be overcome. But why did you, and so many other ascetics before you, locate these passions in the body—in the fleshly part of man? Jesus told us that the man who looks after a woman with lust in his heart commits adultery, that he who hates a man murders him. I am sure you would follow Jesus in this. But the adulterous lust and the murderous hatred he spoke of were surely not of the flesh, but of the spirit, the mind, the will. On this analysis of the human plight, it seems that man's enemy within himself is in his soul, not in his body.

To William James:

It was seventy years ago that you delivered your Gifford Lectures on Natural Religion, which became your great book, *The Varieties of Religious Experience*. Mark Twain's definition of a classic as a book which everybody admires and nobody reads is fortunately not true of this one. The opening statement of Lecture II is one which you could make then with no fear of cavil: "Were one asked to characterize the life of religion in the broadest and most general terms possible, one might say that it consists of the belief that there is an unseen order, and that our supreme good lies in harmoniously adjusting ourselves thereto. This belief and this adjustment are the religious attitude in the soul." Since your time there has developed a strange new gospel (though it has ancient heretical antecedents) to the effect that true religion is not cosmic but social, not adjusting our lives to some unseen order but loving our neighbor. Leigh Hunt's "Abou ben Adhem" would be the patron saint of this new religion if it believed in patron saints. Many profess to be theists but say that all our "God talk" is simply a statement about man. They believe in "God" but only as a word. If they knew their classics they would find a golden text in Pliny the Elder: "God is the helping of man by man, and that is the way to eternal glory." This is a far cry from what you called "the religious attitude." If and when there comes a return to sanity in religion, your statement will make sense to all who share in that resurrection of rationality.

To Karl Marx:

If the Devil is entitled to his due, you are entitled to a fair hearing. The whole world today thinks that you called religion, as such, poisonous dope. What you actually said, you will recall, was this: *"Religious* suffering is at the same time an *expression* of real suffering and a *protest* against real suffering. Religion is the sigh of an oppressed creature, the heart of a heartless world, and the soul of a soulless state of affairs. It is the opium of the people." At least you saw the connection between religion and suffering; you recognized that true religion is always cruciform. An "opium" as you used the term is a medicine that helps one endure pain. My religion, the Christian, is more than that, yet it is that. St. Paul suffered terrible pains for his loyalty to Christ, but he called it all a light affliction which was but for a moment. His love for Christ was what you would call an opium for him. Well, why not? I am sure that Jesus wants his holy religion to be "the heart of a heartless world, and the soul of a soulless state of affairs."

I'm sorry I can't get your full statement on this matter before the whole world. I shall publish this note where a few thousand of the elect will see it. And mind you—though I think you are partly right about the nature of true religion— I think you're wholly wrong about almost everything else.

To Mrs. Karl Marx:

It is reported that near the end of your long and bleak life, you said with a gentle sigh: "How good it would have been if Karl had made some capital instead of writing so much about it!" The village loafer of my childhood was an expert in economics, too. I'm not suggesting that Karl was a loafer. Having just read Robert Payne's biography of him I am much aware of what a beaver he was. But I'm afraid Goethe's Mephistopheles was right when he instructed the student: "My dear young friend, all theory is gray, and the golden tree of life is green." So is the stuff you pay the rent with. I have a feeling that you understood this well but as the dutiful *Hausfrau* of a classic male chauvinist you kept silence. Karl's theories about capital never have worked anywhere. Societies professing Marxist communism survive by being successfully non-Marxist in their economies. Yet Karl made many people think hard about capital, and still does. As an idea man he is not a failure. Nowadays we take better care of people like him by making them professors of economics or special advisers to presidents. It's a pity that you and Karl couldn't have been born a century later.

To Ben Franklin:

At first I was a trifle shocked to learn that you had a good word to speak for vanity. You said that you grew weary of hearing people say, "Without vanity I may say"—and then going on to say some very vain thing. You reflected: "Most people dislike vanity in others, whatever share they may have of it themselves; but I give it fair quarter whenever I meet with it, being persuaded that it is often productive of good to the possessor, and to others who are within his sphere of action; and therefore, in many cases, it would not be altogether absurd if a man were to thank God for his vanity among other comforts of life." I think that by "vanity" you meant what we today mean by "self-respect." If so, I couldn't agree with you more. You were objecting to what had become a fatuous cant word in your day. I wonder what you would have to say about "frankness," a cant word with which we are bludgeoned today. Whenever anybody begins an address to us with "Frankly," we know that something unpleasant is going to follow. It would be more honest for our candid counselor or reporter to begin by saying "Unpleasantly" or "Disagreeably." Nobody ever tells us nice things or good news "frankly." It has got to the point where, frankly, I hate the word.

To John Milton:

Many readers have admired the Devil in *Paradise Lost*. You have been reproached for making him more attractive than your divine Hero. I don't think you have; but you do portray the Devil seriously, and rightly so, for if he exists at all he is no joke or he would not have come as far as he has. In Book IV, when Zephon rebuked him, "abasht the Devil stood, and felt how awful goodness is." Here he stands as the hard-headed realist as contrasted with those softheaded sentimentalists who complain of the dullness of the saint and the charm of the scoundrel. You have to wonder if they have ever seen a real saint or a real scoundrel. Real ones of either sort are not common. Your Devil knows that goodness is as awful as it is rare. When the devils encountered Goodness Incarnate, they screamed in terror. Your countryman C. S. Lewis was sound on this point. He noted "how monotonously alike all the great tyrants and conquerors have been; how gloriously different are the saints." [3] Moreover, when we meet a real one, we usually find him quite "awful" in your sense—awe-inspiring. Your Satan saw the numinous glow in goodness, and shuddered, as well he might.

To Adolf Hitler:

You are commonly called a genius, even by your foes, who vastly outnumber your friends; but the noun is usually preceded by some such adjective as "mad" or "evil." During your last hours, as you recorded for posterity your parting sooth, you said (among many other things): "It requires a genius to make a decision which has not been made already!" My first inclination upon reading this was to agree with you, but then I got to thinking about some of the world's representative geniuses and had to decide against you. When we analyze the great decisions made by geniuses, we find a certain inevitability about them: given the situation, given the total structure of reality, and given the decider, the genius made a decision which had already been made by the God of things as they are. "You cannot compose in consecutive fifths—it is not allowed!" said young Beethoven's teacher. "Beethoven allows it!" replied the budding genius. He was making not your point but mine. The decision that music can be composed in consecutive fifths had already been made by the world's Music Master. Beethoven did not decide it, he discovered what had already been decided. I could give you any number of similar examples, but I have an uneasy feeling that you would not welcome them, unless you have greatly changed—which God grant.

To Lord Acton:

It must be hard to stay where you are, helpless to do anything about it, when the whole world is misquoting you. What you said, of course, was: "Power tends to corrupt, absolute power corrupts absolutely." What the world says you said is "All power corrupts. . . ." Recently I undertook to set the record straight, in public print, as to what Karl Marx actually said about religion as the opium of the people. Now I shall try to do the same for you. Anybody should know that you, a very intelligent man, would never say that all power corrupts. God gives power to some men whom it does not corrupt. Your warning that power *tends* to corrupt is entirely sound; but men are corrupted, not by power or by anything else extraneous to themselves. They are corrupted because they are corruptible, they let themselves be corrupted, they assent to it, they want it.

I wish that more serious thought might be given to the corruption of weakness. We all take for granted (especially we of the weak majority) that the only people who ever grow corrupt are those people with too much power. The misquotation of your dictum has been a golden text for this fallacy. I ask: If the man of power becomes a tyrant and the man of weakness becomes a sycophant, is not the latter corruption as real as the former, and as deplorable?

To Abraham Lincoln:

In your First Inaugural you said: "This country with its institutions belongs to the people who inhabit it. Whenever they shall grow weary of the existing government, they can exercise their constitutional right of amending it, or their revolutionary right to dismember or overthrow it." But then you gave your best and your all to the fight to preserve the Union against those people who asserted that revolutionary right, and I thank God that you did. There is, however, an apparent breach between what you said in the address and what you did as President. Two centuries before you, Sir John Harington truthfully quipped:

> Treason doth never prosper: what's the reason?
> For if it prosper, none dare call it treason.

The conclusion of the matter seems to be that the "right" of a revolution resides solely in its success. The revolutionist who succeeds is a hero and the savior of his country. The revolutionist who fails is a traitor. Because you were not trapped by your own inaugural rhetoric the Union stands to this day. I wish you had never used that phrase "revolutionary right," because it is quoted, with your august authority, by people who have not a trace of your passion for the constitutional right of the people to amend their government.

To Romain Rolland:

I take it that in your day, as now, people talked with terrible facility about sincerity—especially their own. In *Jean Christophe* you wrote: "Least of all could he forgive her lack of sincerity. He did not know that sincerity is a gift as rare as intelligence or beauty and that it cannot justly be expected of everybody." I hear people saying ever so casually: "I don't pretend to be a saint, but at least I'm sincere." You were right: sincerity is a gift as rare as intelligence or beauty, but every cheap jack supposes that he has barrels of it to spare. And sometimes it is found in lunatics. Henry Mencken once reminded us that the man who shot McKinley was undoubtedly sincere. So: we may find sincerity in the fanatic, crank, or monomaniac. We always find it in the saint. And in whom else?

To Hilaire Belloc:

In *The Cruise of the Nona* you wrote: "There was one man upon the deck, smoking a pipe and keeping his mind empty, as is the duty of all mortals in such few intervals of leisure as heaven affords us." You are everlastingly right about that duty of empty-mindedness. Before a mind can receive knowledge or information, it must open up, and to open up is to empty out for the moment. Solomon could well have touched on this in Ecclesiastes 3, saying something like: There is a time to occupy the mind, and a time to empty the mind. Your sailor, blessed was he, knew this, and dutifully observed both times. Some people used to criticize President Eisenhower for the time he spent on the golf course. They were either malicious, or ignorant of the fundamental law of mental respiration, which your sailor had mastered. I am all for statesmen who spend some of their time just wasting it. Such men are much less likely to think their way into Ultimate Solutions for the rest of us. Well did Christopher Morley say of the pre-World War I Germans that the most damning argument against them was that they were not lazy enough. There was grim truth in what Hamlet said to Polonius after killing him: "Thou find'st to be too busy is some danger." It always is.

To Frederick William Faber:

You were both an Englishman and a Victorian, and you often come to my mind when I hear it suggested that one must not look for a sense of humor in an Englishman or a Victorian. I recall what you said in your last hour as you lay in mortal agony. You had already received the Last Sacraments that day, but you lived longer than expected, and toward the end you asked for the Last Sacraments again. When this request was denied, you sighed, "Well, if I can't have the Last Sacraments, give me Pickwick!" So, thanks to Charles Dickens, your holy death was a happy one.

I am neither an Englishman nor a Victorian, but when I need spiritual mirth, I know where to look for it. It's very likely to be in Dickens, or Gilbert & Sullivan, or perhaps in our still-living late-Victorian Mr. Wodehouse.

God rested you merry in your last hour. I pray for a holy death, with the understanding that to be holy it must be happy. And how can man die better than with a chuckle?

To Bernard of Cluny:

One of your great Latin hymns is known to us as "Jerusalem the Golden." Recently a clergyman blasted it, in a sermon. It is my duty as a reporter to tell you what he said and my pleasure as a man to reject it as prissy nonsense. He concentrated his ire on these lines:

> There is the throne of David,
> And there, from care released,
> The shout of them that triumph,
> The song of them that feast.

He rails against this eternal singing and eating; your idea of Heaven is practically his idea of Hell. Well, my dear twelfth-century brother in Christ, I hope you are right about Heaven and that by God's mercy I shall join you and the other concelebrants conjubilant with song. It is rumored that when Theodore Roosevelt reorganized the heavenly choir, he ordered 100,000 each of sopranos, altos, and tenors, then announced that he himself would take the bass. My dream is of taking the tenor. And about the food: Enrico Caruso and Mme. Ernestine Schumann-Heink were devoted dining companions. To sing like them one must eat like them, *n'est-ce pas?* One night he found her about to eat a steak so huge that even he goggled. "Stina," he asked, "are you going to eat that big steak all alone?" "Nein," she replied modestly, "mit potatoes."

I get my idea of what the Master of the Feast wants, as Host, from reading about what He liked as Guest (John 2:1-11). If that preacher wants to spend eternity on a songless diet, I leave him to his dream, but shouldn't he leave me to mine? I cannot aspire to anything higher than what you describe so attractively.

To Reinhold Niebuhr:

Nearly forty years ago you attended a Christmas Eucharist in a great cathedral. The stuffy and complacent sermon by the Bishop almost ruined it for you, but the liturgy of the Book of Common Prayer redeemed it. In the sermon there was nothing of the godly penitence which was expressed in the General Confession: "We acknowledge and bewail our manifold sins and wickedness, which we, from time to time, most grievously have committed, by thought, word, and deed, against thy divine majesty, provoking most justly thy wrath and indignation against us." You felt that there should be this note in what Christians say to God when they celebrate their redemption. If you have influence in Heaven, I hope you will ask for some kind of celestial restraining order upon the people down here who are trying to "purge" our traditional liturgies of what they consider excessively penitential elements. St. Jerome once recalled how he had tried to think up some suitable offering to make to the Christ Child as a birthday gift at Christmas, and the Holy Child said to him: "It is your sins that I want, Jerome. Give them to me so that I can forgive them." That, you felt, is what Christmas is all about. The Prayer Book liturgy helped you to make such a heart-offering to the Lord. I feel that you share my hope that the people of God will not be robbed of this goodly heritage.

To Herbert Spencer:

To your everlasting credit you were one of the first to see that we must find some way of dealing with malefactors that is not merely, purely punitive. It was eighty years ago that you formulated this principle: "Absolute morality is the regulation of conduct in such a way that pain shall not be inflicted." By your choice of the adjective "absolute" you tacitly recognized that your ideal is an ideal, not wholly attainable in this world as it is. I suppose that the pain you had in mind was the pain deliberately inflicted by the punisher as a means of visiting the sin upon the flesh of the sinner.

But I wonder how much this helps the judge on his bench, the parent of the naughty child, or the good soul at the hard job of regulating his own conduct. What he has got to do is usually, if not always, something that is painful, however good the final end may be. You know that in this life as it is, down here on this probationary planet, there is no growth without pains.

Even so, unless our realism is richly permeated by your idealism, we can only continue to be savages—and futile as well—in our treatment of our erring brothers and our own erring selves. Your absolute morality is absolutely right.

To Samuel Butler:

I respectfully beg to differ. In your apology for the Devil, you ask us to remember that we have heard only one side of the case: "God has written all the books." Has he indeed? What if, as I think is true, the Devil has written many of them (by remote control) and has signed God's name to them? What is indisputable is that neither God nor the Devil has actually written the books, but men. And many a man who has written what was meant to be a godly treatise has been trying to serve two Masters while doing so. Let's say that he has written a book of theology to the greater glory of God—as is written right there on the flyleaf, so who can doubt it?—but also in the hope that all the people who matter will be talking about his genius, "lost in wonder, love, and praise" not only for God but also for God's inspired interpreter. Well now: Who *did* write that book? Not the Devil, perhaps; but will you seriously maintain that it was God?

To Thomas Betterton:

I know two things about you. You were an actor who died in 1710, and you said: "Actors speak of things imaginary as if they were real, while preachers too often speak of things real as if they were imaginary." We preachers have always been tempted and inclined to do this. Because I preach and have been justly criticized for this fault I think as hard and well as I can about the question: How can preachers speak of real things as if they were real? Undoubtedly the complete answer to the question contains a number of things, but I'm sure of one of them. The late Professor Helen C. White, in her searching study of the seventeenth-century metaphysical poets, analyzed John Donne's hypnotically powerful preaching. She noted that he preached *to himself first.* In the words of the Puritan Richard Baxter, he preached "as a dying man to dying men." He preached to himself, in the hearing of others. This isn't the whole answer, by any means, but it's an unexceptionable part of the whole answer. We who preach should never omit ourselves from our audience. If it isn't Gospel for me, how can it be Gospel for anybody else?

To Thomas Arnold:

In 1828, upon your appointment to the headmastership of Rugby, you wrote to a friend: "My object will be, if possible, to form Christian men, for Christian boys I can scarcely hope to make." I wish all modern Christian educationists knew their Christianity, their men, and their boys half as well as you did. You saw, with Tertullian, that Christians are made, not born: made by God's grace and by their own earnest, life-long striving. Karl Barth, who came a century after you, said that "strictly speaking, there are no Christians; there is only the eternal possibility of becoming Christians." This, I am sure, is exactly what you had in mind. You saw your own self as, in Barth's sense, a pre-Christian. Some critic called Dickens's Oliver Twist "that freak of nature—a Christian boy." It is a just verdict. I find the lad simply unbelievable; yes, and I love children, as you did, too, or you would never have become the immortal schoolmaster.

You hold, as I understand you, that education in Christ is education for eternity, that the holiest saint at the age of ninety is not yet out of the nursery stage.

So far as I can see, there has been no change in the ground rules of the game of eternal life since your day. You are still right.

To Martin Buber:

It's odd, and I think profoundly promising, that in today's religious thought and concern there is so much talk about holiness. Odd it is, because one would expect a generation that exalts "sacred secularity" and "religionless Christianity" to find the word "holy" ridiculous or abhorrent. I think it means simply that *homo religiosus* cannot find rest except in the Holy, or at least in his own search and longing for the Holy. Like all ultimately real things, holiness is beyond our definition; but anybody who ponders this statement of yours will see, or sense, what holiness is: "There is no not-holy, there is only that which has not yet been hallowed, which has not yet been redeemed to its holiness."

To Francis Bacon:

Yes, we are, as you put it, "much beholden to Machiavel and others, that write what men do, and not what they ought to do." History should not be homily. But don't you agree that we are even more beholden to those men who tell us what we *ought* to do—if they know what they are talking about? Thomas Henry Huxley was another illustrious Englishman, who came three centuries after you. He said: "If some great Power would agree to make me always think what is true and do what is right, on condition of being turned into a sort of clock and wound up every morning before I got out of bed, I should instantly close with the offer." I think I know why you said what you did about our debt to the candid and objective historians. You were weary of pious propaganda as a substitute for accurate information about what men do. We are indeed in sorry shape when that is all that we get in place of sound history. But you are a wise man, so I trust you agree that the good moralist serves us at least as well as the good historian. We need both.

To King Solomon:

What a sly, laconic way you had of describing greedy men! —"They lay wait for their own blood; they lurk privily for their own lives" (Proverbs 1:18). The art of language has hideously deteriorated since your time; it is as if we needed three thousand years more, of unremitting effort, to learn to write as badly as we do. A modern master of American idiom would need at least two or three hundred words to say what you said in your five Hebrew words (fourteen in our familiar English translation). He would tell us how the obsessively acquisitive man is a menace not only to society as a whole, but most of all to his own self. He would come on in wave upon wave of puffing verbiage, earnestly contending that self-aggrandizement is a form of self-destruction and that the profit motive is a manifestation of the death wish. All you needed was a few words about men ambushing themselves. And Hebrew wasn't supposed to be a language for subtlety and irony. I wish I knew the cause of this sorrowful mystery. Perhaps it's because writing is too easy for us. I can sit down at this typewriter and bat out thousands of words by the hour. Writing was a much more laborious business for you ancients. You had to make every word count, and so you did. In the art of writing, it seems that—as our Wordsworth put it in another connection—the child is father of the man.

To John Kendrick Bangs:

As a poet you fell somewhat short of the *crème de la crème* rank of Milton and Keats, but this bit of counsel to God got you into Bartlett's:

I think mankind by thee would be less bored
If only thou wert not thine own reward.

I suspect that God himself liked your cheek but that some of his elect were not amused. My only trouble is with your theology. On the facing page in Bartlett's is a comment by G. Lowes Dickinson, on a very different subject, that contains implicitly the answer to you. Talking about Chinese poetry he says: "It contemplates life just as it presents itself, without any veil of ideas, any rhetoric or sentiment; it simply clears away the obstruction which habit has built up between us and the beauty of things." What he calls "the beauty of things" is God as emotionally and esthetically experienced by us. Suppose that you and I are gazing enraptured at a sunset over the Dakota prairie at that time of year when the wheat is ready for harvest and there's a golden haze in the air through which the sun's rays filter. Our rapture is our reward for simply taking the trouble to look at it. But our rapture is in God; we are enjoying him in this manifestation of the divine Beauty. You needed a dash of mysticism. It might have improved your poetry; it would certainly have improved your theology and enhanced your joy of living.

To Moshe Leib Sassover:

I learned who you are by reading an anthology of Hasidic literature. You used to attend all the sick children in your city, and you once said: "He who cannot suck the matter from the boils of a child sick with the plague has not yet gone halfway up the height of love for his fellow men." I don't know how it was in your day, but in my day people (whether Jew or Gentile) speak very easily of the importance of loving our fellow men. There isn't nearly so much talk about loving God—about what Jesus called the First and Great Commandment. This easy talk about loving people expresses an easy concept based upon an unexamined assumption that it's always easy to love anybody if one will just try. Thus we readily conclude that a check for $10, or $1,000 if we can give it without hurting, to some organized charity is the last word in grade-A loving, for which we get both a moral credit with God and a tax deduction with IRS.

What we need are some reminders like yours of what is involved in loving somebody as God commands us to love. You say: "Can you suck the pus from the boils of a plague victim if that is the task at hand? If so, you show some comprehension of what God's command really means and calls for. Otherwise, don't trifle with God's truth; don't call whatever else you are doing 'love.'"

I'm afraid you knew what you were talking about.

68

To St. Augustine of Hippo:

Among all your thousands of felicitous phrases, one of my favorites is your reference to the Ten Commandments as "that psaltery of ten strings" (*psalterium decem chordarum*, Confessions III.8). Like the author of Psalm 119, you heard the music of Heaven in the Law of God: "Thy statutes have been my song, in the house of my pilgrimage" (Psalm 119:54). Christians today have fallen into the disastrous habit of setting Love against Law, as if these were not contrapuntal but antipodal. The preachers of this strange doctrine tell us that we should serve the Lord out of love rather than because he commands it. I cannot imagine what they make of this mandate of Jesus: "If you love me, keep my commandments" (John 14:15). What you understood so well, and they do not, is that our only way of loving God *is* to obey him. How else? Can we give him anything he needs and doesn't have? Love makes obedience a pleasure, as when Jacob served seven years for Rachel because of the love he had for her. But the converse is also true: As we obey the Lord our love for him grows while we progressively discover how loving a master he is.

To Alfred, Lord Milner:

You died in 1925, but I don't know just when it was that you said: "The last thing which the thought of the Empire inspires in me is a desire to boast—to wave a flag, or to shout 'Rule Britannia.' When I think of it, I am much more inclined to go into a corner by myself and pray." I imagine that it was about the time, around the turn of this century, when the Spanish-American world citizen George Santayana said, of the British Empire: "Never since the heroic days of Greece has the world had such a sweet, just, boyish master. It will be a black day for the human race when scientific blackguards, conspirators, churls and fanatics manage to supplant him!"

He may have been unusually fortunate in his contacts with the Empire; he must have known some imperialists like yourself. I can tell you, in case you are not in a position to observe, that though your Empire has been liquidated, and we are assured that this is progress, there are millions of people in lands which once belonged to the Empire who would be a thousandfold happier in every way if they could exchange places with their grandparents who lived under the Union Jack.

Progress is a baffling, enigmatic thing, isn't it? It seems to me that we have progress only when we have men of your spirit managing our earthly kingdoms: servants of the Most High God, and so servants of all men.

To Malcolm X:

"Time and time again," you declared, "the black, the brown, the red, and the yellow races have witnessed and suffered the white man's small ability to understand the simple notes of the spirit. The white man seems tone deaf to the total orchestration of humanity." It was inevitable, just, and right that you should have felt this way. You appeal to history, to the facts of past and present. I would appeal to something deeper than history. The white oppressors and exploiters are what they are, not because they are white but because they are people. A man's race is a fact deeply rooted in his being, but his soul lies deeper—and that's where all trouble begins. You would cure white men of their whiteness if you could, and I can't blame you for wishing that you could; but I'm afraid that the result would be terribly disappointing, if that's all that you did with them. What you would still have is that heart of man which, as Jeremiah said long ago, is desperately wicked. And no race of men is less, or more, contaminated than the others. Yours is a defensive racism, merely retaliatory, and it can accomplish nothing. We are all tone deaf to the total orchestration of humanity until we are born again of the Spirit. The healing of the nations and of the races begins in common repentance and regeneration by the power of God.

To John Donne:

I'm sure that in your day many Christians were tempted to a false spirituality, and so you wrote:

> From thinking us all soule, neglecting thus
> Our mutual duties, Lord deliver us.

Our problem is somewhat different today, although if we look for them we can still find people who think themselves all soul. However, most of the Christian illuminati in 1972 are little inclined to that error, to the neglect of bodies. They are tempted rather to think themselves "all heart" about the needs of human bodies, forgetting that people are souls who have bodies and not bodies that may or may not have souls. One text that is not overpreached in today's churches is, "Man does not live by bread alone." I can testify that it has been a very long time since I met a Christian so superspiritual that he forgot his own body, to say nothing of the body of poor Lazarus at his gate. I believe that if you were here among us in the flesh today you would feel moved to admonish us about the danger of thinking ourselves "all heart" because we have a tender feeling for bodies, while forgetting that our soul may this night be required of us. I'm not forgetting the final truth of this whole soul-body matter: that if you're going to love and help some person you must love and help him "all over," not just in his body or just in his soul. What's bothering me is the "all-heart" heresy.

To Thomas à Kempis:

Dr. Samuel Johnson said that your book must be a good one because the world has opened its arms to receive it. He obviously had not read it himself, and the reason he gives for praising it is very odd—especially coming from him, since he was no democrat in his literary taste or in anything else. His friend Boswell dealt better with you: he actually read you, and in his *Life of Johnson* gave his rather free translation of one of your finest precepts (in Bk. I, chap. 16): "Be not angry that you cannot make others as you wish them to be, since you cannot make yourself as you wish to be." Although I have read all of the *Imitation* before, and in fact first read it very many years ago, this particular word of the Lord spoken through you never really "grabbed" me, as we say today, until just now when I read it in Boswell. I'm sorry this is so, because I have had need of it through all the days of my years to date. I'm an old hand at making others as I wish them to be—that is, wishing that I could. My efforts to make myself as I wish to be have been less than epoch-making. Well—better late than never. I can use this precept for whatever time is left to me, and try to give it some circulation. Truer words were never spoken, and nobody ever spoke them better than you, except, of course, the Word himself (Matthew 7:3-5).

To Jean Vianney, the Curé d'Ars:

About repentance, you said in four words (*C'est toujours à recommencer*) what couldn't be said so well in volumes: "To repent is always to start over again." You probably never heard the story about your English contemporary Thomas Carlyle and what happened to the first draft of his opus on the French Revolution. He had spent ten years of travail upon it, and when he had finished the manuscript, of which he had made no copy, he gave it to his friend John Stuart Mill for a critical reading. Mill placed it on a mantel over a fireplace, intending to start reading it the next morning. But a housemaid got to it before he did, thought it was scrap paper, and used it all to start a fire. When Mill had to tell him what had happened, Carlyle paled and said nothing. That night he wrote in his diary: "It was as if my Invisible Schoolmaster had torn up my copybook when I showed it to him and had said, 'No, boy, thou must write it better!'" Sometimes God says to a man, not about his sin but about his work and labor of love: "No, boy, thou must write it better!" *C'est toujours à recommencer.*

To St. Paul the Apostle:

I hope that what you say in I Corinthians 9:9 is simply a lapse. There, in arguing that ministers of the Gospel have a right to be supported, you quote Deuteronomy 25:4: "You shall not muzzle the ox while it is treading out the corn." Your point is that if the useful ox earns his food so does the minister of Christ. If only you had stopped with that rather ingenious textual clincher! But then you asked: "Does God care for oxen?" Your question implies that he does not, and that the Deuteronomy text properly refers not to dumb beasts but to Christian ministers. It's hard to understand how you, so great a Jew and Christian, could so misread this word of God. The Holy Spirit inspired those humane provisions in Deuteronomy for the care of animals; surely you knew this. Your Master taught that not a sparrow falls to the ground without the Father. "Does God care for sparrows?" I would guess that in your intense concern for the material needs of the ministers of Christ, you didn't think through the implications of your reference to God and the oxen. I'm afraid that your statement has done grave harm to the Christian movement for the humane treatment of animals. This you never intended, I'm sure, and only part of the fault is yours. The rest belongs to Christians who attribute to your every word an inerrancy you never dreamt of claiming for yourself. I hope you will agree with me that the blessed Apostle St. Paul is wrong about God and the oxen.

To Ralph Waldo Emerson:

You had a remarkable love-hate affair with the Christian ministry. In one of your 1832 Journal entries you wrote: "I sometimes thought that, in order to be a good minister, it was necessary to leave the ministry." Today, 140 years later, many good ministers share your feeling, and some are doing just that—leaving the ministry. The profession is even more antiquated than it was in your day. Professional educators, social workers, counselors, psychiatrists today do for people what ministers of religion used to do, and often do these services better than the clergy ever could. But is "helping people" the ultimate essence of the ministry? Or is it rather representative priesthood—the minister being God's man to us and our man to God? Suppose that this Christian priestliness is the one thing needful in ministry. Antiquated it may be. But then, what truly indispensable thing is *not* antiquated? Religion itself; marriage; the effort to be civilized, especially the exhausting effort to keep reason and conscience in control over the passions—but why go on? All are antiquated, none is dispensable. Somerset Maugham said that all great truths are too important to be new. Of course he was right. All the great human and humanizing institutions are too important to be new, and important enough to be antiquated: the ministry included. Hopelessly antiquated it is—but so is Christ our Great High Priest. God seems to use the antiquated things to confound the wise.

To Walter Bagehot:

A hundred years ago you were melancholy as you reflected whether the benevolence of mankind, such as it is, on the whole does more good than harm. Today, the question is still moot, after all these ages, and men of honest and good heart have continuing cause for melancholy about it. A typical example: Following World War I there were many German orphans, and many benevolent Norwegians who had compassion on them and adopted them. Some of these youngsters, having grown up—or down—returned to Germany and by betraying their foster parents helped the Nazi thugs to infiltrate and subjugate Norway. Benevolence is well known for such faithful failures as this.

But there—I called it a failure, as if I knew whereof I speak. Don't we go wrong on this matter by looking for results in the wrong area—that of the immediate, the visible, the obvious? Any action, be it benevolent or whatever, has eternal consequences, everlasting effects upon all whom it affects in any way. Therefore it is ridiculous to suppose that we, being always *in medias res*, can make an assessment that is final or even accurate. If God is, and God is God, we can knock off our melancholy about this reflection, and, indeed, knock off the reflection itself, if what it consists of is doubting and fearing.

To James Russell Lowell:

There are moments when I envy your genial theology as expressed in this statement: "I take great comfort in God. I think he is sometimes much amused at the human race, but on the whole he loves us. He would never have let us get at the match-box if he had not known that the frame-work of the universe is fire-proof." Living as you did in the pre-Atomic Age, you had no way of knowing that the framework of the universe is not in fact fire-proof. Since your time, God has let us get at a box containing matches that could blow us all up.

I, too, take great comfort in God, but I'm not sure that your comfort and mine are the same. Mine is austere where yours is sunny. My comfort is that if somebody blows up the planet, God will still be here, and that we who are his beloved children will still be his beloved children—but we shall not still be "here," and I like it here.

And I must submit that you overestimate God's amusement at us and that you underestimate his love for us when you say "on the whole" he loves us. If he didn't love us more than on the whole, on balance, we should have been long dead, gone, and forgotten as a bad experiment. And I don't think God is *ever* amused at us. He laughs with us when there's something to laugh about, but he loves us too much to find us amusing. You were a father. You found monkeys and kittens amusing, but never your children after they were supposed to have grown up.

To Martin Luther:

You loved a lusty belly laugh and I daresay you still do. Please don't stop me if you've heard this one:

A Hollywood movie producer was insufferably conceited about his knowledge of old books and first editions. Some people who had had enough of it brought to Hollywood an actor, unknown to this producer, who appeared as a country doctor from Iowa. The two men were introduced at a cocktail party and the conversation was brought around to old books.

"Personally, I hate them," said the "doctor." "I can't stand their smell when they get all mouldy. Just the other day I threw one out—an old German Bible that had been in our family for generations."

"An old German Bible?" asked the expert. "Do you happen to remember who printed it?"

"Let's see. I think it was G-u-t-e—*Guten* somebody or other."

"Not *Gutenberg!*" screamed the sage. "You fool, you've thrown away a fortune! We must fly back to Iowa at once and rescue it if we possibly can."

"Don't get excited," said the "doctor" casually. "That old Bible can't be worth anything no matter who printed it. Some character named Martin Luther had scribbled his name all over it."

To Thomas Hardy:

I forget from which one of your novels I excerpted this reflection: "It is the on-going of the world that produces its sadness. If the world stood still at a felicitous moment, there would be no sadness in it. The sun and the moon standing still on Ajalon was not a catastrophe for Israel, but a type of Paradise." This is not popular doctrine today. Contemporary culture is fatuously devoted to change as a glorious end and good in itself, but I am convinced that you are right about the cause of sadness and the conditions of happiness. The latter can perfectly exist only in a better world than this present one, where "change and decay in all around" we see. The three companions of Jesus who went up into the Mount of Transfiguration with him wanted to capture and freeze that felicitous moment forever. Who can blame them? They knew when they were happy. Of course there is another condition of happiness, in human life in this temporal stage; as J. B. Yeats put it: "We are happy when we are growing." Growth is change for the better in our own being; but the change that saddens us is rather that "on-going of the world" of which you spoke. Jesus and his companions could not remain in that felicitous moment; they had to come down to the world of changes and chances, and crucifixions. I will not say that that necessity was bad; I say only that it was sad. It always is. I like to think of Heaven as the blessed haven from all on-goingness: the felicitous moment of seeing the King in his beauty, and this made permanent.

To Ralph Waldo Emerson:

From your Journals: "Every loafer knows the way to the rum shop, but every angel does not know the way to his nectar." You raise a tremendous question, and I don't blame you for not staying to answer it. Why does the loafer *en route* to the rum shop make the angel *en route* to his nectar resemble a retarded (lobotomized) rat in a new maze? It cannot be a difference in innate intelligence. Some "angels" (people with heavenly aspirations) are geniuses, some loafers are imbeciles.

I suggest that what makes the difference is a combination of two things: *interest* and *craft*. The loafer wants that rum with all his heart, soul, mind, and strength. As the football coaches say, "He gives you 150%." Too often the angel on the way to his nectar is the man who wants to go to Heaven —but not tonight. Then, craft. This ought to be a good word rather than a bad one for Christians. A priest should work hard at his priestcraft, and the layman at his laycraft, for craft is the art of doing a job in the best possible way. Somebody said of your angel sort of person:

> He tried to paint a black cat white,
> He tried to lure a moth with camphor.
> He made an honest, hopeless fight
> For things he didn't care a damphor.

There, I've at least tried to answer the question you raised, which is more than you did.

81

To Dr. Samuel Johnson:

Your effort to define happiness strikes me as more successful than your effort to practice it. To refresh your memory (as if it ever needed refreshing!): Hume had said that all who are happy are equally happy; the little Miss with the new gown at the dancing-school ball, the general leading his victorious army, and so on. Boswell quoted Hume to you, and your response was thundering. A peasant and a philosopher may be equally *satisfied*, you said, but not equally *happy*. Then you gave your admirable definition: "Happiness consists in the multiplicity of agreeable consciousness." (A modern variant of your essential idea runs: "Happiness is a warm puppy.") Then Boswell quoted, *contra* Hume, the *aperçu* of one Rev. Mr. Robert Brown: "A small drinking-glass and a large one may be equally full; but the large one holds more than the small." It is a matter of personal capacity for happiness, and in this no two of us are equal. But I'm not sure you are right in assuming that a peasant is inferior in his capacity to a philosopher. As I see them, the philosophers down through the ages have not been a conspicuously jolly lot. The capacity for happiness is more in the spiritual dimension; in your juxtaposition of peasant with philosopher you seem to make it merely intellectual. And you leave unanswered the question: Why should a man of both intellectual and spiritual eminence fall short of happiness? As an example I might instance one Samuel Johnson.

To Gilbert Keith Chesterton:

You searched diligently for a sound reason-for-being of the literary critic, but if your last word on this was what you wrote in your Introduction to *Old Curiosity Shop,* I am both disappointed and aghast. "Criticism," you said, "does not exist to say about authors the things that they know themselves. It exists to say the things about them which they did not know themselves." Say it isn't so—*you,* putting the critic in the analyst's chair and the author on the couch? It turns out to be as bad as I feared, for you went on to say: "The function of criticism, if it has a legitimate function at all, can only be one function—that of dealing with the subconscious part of the author's mind, which only the critic can express, and not the conscious part of the author's mind, which the author himself can express. Either criticism is no good at all (a very defensible position) or else criticism means saying about an author the very things that would have made him jump out of his boots." I love and revere you, dear GKC, but perhaps you did write too much. Here you are, commissioning critics to play God to their betters. It wasn't one of your better days. The perfect prayer for the critic is in Psalm 19: "Keep thy servant also from presumptuous sins, lest they get the dominion over me; so shall I be undefiled, and innocent from the great offense."

To William Morris:

I'm afraid that I have just blown my stack at my dearly beloved Gilbert Chesterton for having expressed a view of the critic's role which would discredit the rankest barbarian. I don't know what possessed him to say it: to the effect that the critic is to tell the world what the author was *really* saying, as distinct from what the poor blunderbus thought he was saying. If this is a slight caricature of what he said, it isn't far off the mark, and it's what I hear him saying. When I think of a competent critic, talking like one, my mind turns to you and your superb rage when you were shown some sculptural monstrosity: "I could have gnawed it better with my teeth!" You didn't concern yourself with what you imagined the sculptor was trying to say; you dealt with what he did say. In your sight it was an abomination of desolations, and you said so with a splendor that would become at least a minor Olympian deity. "I could have gnawed it better with my teeth!" That is honest-to-God criticism— and memorable literature in the bargain. People today have a vulgar phrase for a high virtue, the constitutive virtue of sound criticism: "telling it like it is" (as the critic sees it, of course). You told it like it was, as William Morris saw it.

To Amos the Prophet:

To you it seemed self-evident that nations, like individuals, live if they walk in God's way and die if they do not: "If disaster falls on a city, has not the Lord been at work?" (Amos 3:6b, NEB.)

A recent commentator is rather patronizing about your willingness "to argue from moral facts to political conclusions." He minces: "It would be reassuring if history could be shown to exhibit a consistent moral purpose, but such a pattern is difficult to demonstrate convincingly." [4] Perhaps so—if all that one is looking at is history itself. But our difficulty in seeing "consistent moral purpose" in history may be partly due to "the dullness of our blinded sight." As *you* looked at history, you listened to the voice of history's Lord. When people do that listening, along with their looking, they begin to see the hand of God in the affairs of men. It was such a listener-seer who once predicted that Napoleon's glory days were numbered because the man had become a nuisance to God. One must have some firsthand knowledge of God before one can see that a man or nation is a nuisance to him. Another man who shared your vision called history "God's roaring loom." That says it all. We begin to understand history as we begin to know history's God. "Though the mills of God grind slowly, yet they grind exceeding small." And, as you correctly noted, they don't always grind so very slowly.

To William Law:

One does not turn to your *Serious Call* for "exciting" reading; but last night I was reading you while in bed, and I came upon this passage which kept me awake for a while translating it into contemporary terms: "More people are kept from a true sense and state of religion by a regular kind of sensuality and indulgence than by gross drunkenness. More men live regardless of the great duties of piety through too great a concern for worldly goods than through direct injustice." In present-day language it comes out like this: "More people are kept from the Christ-life by their passion for Country Club life than by alcoholism; more live 'without God in the world' through bondage to 'security' than through crime." This is pretty strong talk to us who want "all this, and Heaven too"—in that order. If you had been a gloomy fanatic we could write you off as such, but you were not. And your divine Master talked the same way long before you, as when he said that whores and tax-grafters enter the kingdom of God before some other people. Henceforth I shall not recommend you to anybody as good bedtime reading. But you are a first-rate awakener, being the true Gospel man that you are.

To Dag Hammarskjöld:

You gave us a proverb worthy of everlasting remembrance when you said: "In our era, the road to holiness necessarily passes through the world of action." You meant, I'm sure, that in our age it is not enough for the aspirant to holiness (wholeness of being) to be a mere theoretician of life or a contemplative. None of the great masters of the spiritual life in times past would disagree with you, at least not any Jews or Christians. Even so antiworldly a saint as Jerome was a man of tireless and titanic action. I hope nobody understands you to be announcing some new law for "our era." And I hope nobody understands you to be saying that "activism"—just sheer doing something all the time for the sake of doing something—is the road to holiness, for I know you meant nothing of the sort. Your proverb should be read along with St. Teresa's: "To give our Lord a perfect hospitality, Mary and Martha must combine." I find evidence, in *Markings*, of the Mary mind in you, and I am certain that you would want to be so understood.

To Anonymous:

I mean you, good Sir or lovely Lady, who *ca.* A.D. 1300 wrote this verse:

> Ich am of Irlaunde,
> Ant of the holy londe
>   Of Irlande.
> Gode sire, pray ich the,
> For of saynte charité,
> Come ant daunce wyth me
>   In Irlaunde.

It's memorable verse and true religion. In a holy land people dance for joy in the Lord, and if one has holy charity he will join in the dance. If your invitation still stands, I will gladly accept it as soon as circumstances permit, and I pray that they will one day—though it may be elsewhere than Ireland; and you will have a terribly clumsy pupil on your hands, or your feet. Three hundred years after you, Bishop Jeremy Taylor of the Church of England expressed the same truth about holiness and happiness in prose worthy to be remembered alongside your poetry. I'm sure you will like what he said even though he was an Englishman: "Now our duty standeth on the sunny side. For so good a God do we serve, he hath made it our duty to be happy, so that we cannot please him unless we be infinitely pleased ourselves."

To Sir James Barrie:

Evidently you were in a sad mood when you wrote: "The life of every man is a diary in which he means to write one story and writes another, and his humblest hour is when he compares the volume as it is with what he vowed to make it." Yes. But that humblest hour can be the prelude to his finest hour, depending upon whether he is a Peter or a Judas. One man repents and lives, the other despairs and dies. Christian preachers throughout this age of grace have been warning us that we must repent, and indeed we must. But they should proclaim at least as emphatically the good news from Heaven that we *can* repent. Even the pagan Marcus Aurelius saw the divine wonder of it, and exclaimed as if dazed by joy: "You can begin a new life!" And so I think we need to be both sad and glad about the fact of which you speak: sad about our failure to write the story we had vowed to write, but glad that the Holy Spirit of God is, as they say in today's theater, "waiting in the wings" to give us the fresh start and the new life. And every faithful and persevering Christian who ever lived a fairly long life could tell you, from his own experience, that the story you write in Diary B will be a better one than you ever dreamt of writing in Diary A if you let the Master of Life write it through you.

To Henri Frédéric Amiel:

Rejoice that you do not live in this age of sensitivity training and "openness." Your advocacy of modesty (*pudeur*) would bring scorn upon you. Exactly 120 years to the day after you wrote this entry in your Journal, I am pondering it: "Modesty is always the sign and safeguard of a mystery. It is explained by its contrary—profanation. Shyness or modesty is, in truth, the half-conscious sense of a secret of nature or of the soul too intimately individual to be given or surrendered. It is *exchanged*. To surrender what is most profound and mysterious in one's being and personality at any price less than that of absolute reciprocity is profanation." What you call profanation, Voltaire calls boredom: "The secret of being a bore is to tell everything." You are both right. What you call *pudeur* suggests what we call in English *reserve* and *reverence*. This element in human relations is condemned today by those who would have us strip naked whenever we meet. Their technique both bores and profanes. Unto God alone are all hearts open and all desires known, which is as it ought to be. In one of Robert Frost's poems, a man says: "Good fences make good neighbors." I agree with him, with you, and with Voltaire, and I modestly suggest that together we agree with our Creator who so made us. Without fences we cannot be neighbors. Without *pudeur* we cannot be persons with one another. Mutual stripping, like other kinds of prostitution, leads not to mutual love but to mutual and self-contempt.

To Arthur James Balfour:

You simply couldn't have meant it when (or if) you said: "Biography should be written by an acute enemy." Somebody once quoted you as having said this; maybe he was an enemy of yours. If so, my point needs no further exposition: you see what happens when an enemy writes *your* biography—he lies. A man's biography should show us the man himself. To ask that it tell *nothing but the truth* is to ask too much of any mortal work, but it must strive at least to tell *the whole truth,* and this no enemy can ever do. Only love sees any person as he is, only love can tell the whole truth of the person. If you never said this, or have been misquoted, I apologize. It's this stupid statement I'm attacking. Whoever actually said it either knows nothing or cares nothing about serious and honest biography.

To Julia Ward Howe:

All our reasons for remembering you are complimentary. I'm especially grateful for the fine spontaneous theology from your lips that day when you invited crusading abolitionist Senator Charles Sumner to dinner to meet some of your friends. He declined, saying "Really, Julia, I have lost all interest in individuals," and you replied: "Why Charles! God hasn't got as far as that yet." I'm sure that Sumner was in his own way great and good. He saw the slaves as an oppressed race, and he fought for their liberty as if it were his own. But he did not see them, feel them, as individual persons. Or perhaps he did—but failed to see others as individuals. Some of the world's best men, and somewhat fewer of the world's best women, have shared this defect. Today we have some valiantly compassionate people who fight the good fight for some class or group or cause but have sunk into that Sumnerian disinterest in individuals. It seems especially strange, and sad, that any follower of Jesus Christ should make this mistake, with the example of their Master so clearly in front of them. Perhaps they are too busy to look occasionally at their Paradigm.

To the Editor of the Harrisburg Patriot and Union in 1863:

Poor fellow, you are remembered as the editor who dismissed Lincoln's Gettysburg Address as "the silly remarks of the President." I have a word of small comfort for you as you do your eternal penance of memory. I, too, am an editor, and very opinionated. Sometimes, as my fingers tremble in midair over my typewriter while I premeditate editorial mayhem, I remember two people to my own admonition and restraint. One is Gamaliel, who once said of a very controversial movement in his day: "Refrain from these men, and let them alone: for if this counsel or this work be of men, it will come to nought: but if it be of God, ye cannot overthrow it . . ." (Acts 5:38-39). The other is you. Your mistake is a red-light beacon.

Another bit of small comfort—the best I can come up with, and offered with sincere sympathy: Do you know what the *Edinburgh Review* said of John Keats's poetry when it appeared? "This will never do." Your offense is not solitary, and you are not alone.

To Roger Williams:

On January 1, 1666, you wrote to the village of Warwick: "Let us not soothe and sing ourselves to sleep with murdering lullabies: let us provide for changes and by timely humiliation prevent them." Three centuries separate your idiom from ours, and I want to be sure that I understand you, so let me run over your words with you. "Lullabies" are self-administered tranquilizers in which we tell ourselves that we're doing beautifully. Right? By providing for changes you mean preparing for bad consequences tomorrow of any mess we make today. Right? We can prevent such changes by "timely humiliation"—your most arresting phrase. I take it to mean a faithful obedience of the will of God in all things today. Thus, if we white settlers of Warwick deal fraternally with our Indian neighbors today, there will be no calamitous change tomorrow in our presently peaceful relations with them. In our idiom "humiliation" means shame and failure. In yours, it evidently meant being wise as serpents and harmless as doves; humiliation meant humility, down-to-earth good sense, honest-to-God good living. Right? You are well remembered as an eloquent example of what it means to be a free man under God.

To Dr. Samuel Johnson:

You tried to set Mr. Erskine's mind at rest about a scripture that troubled him—the account of the angel of the Lord's smiting 185,000 Assyrians in one night. I quote you, as quoted by Boswell: "Sir, you should recollect that there was a supernatural interposition; they were destroyed by pestilence. You are not to suppose that the angel of the Lord went about and stabbed each of them with a dagger, or knocked them on the head, man by man." Evidently you felt that the angel must do the job in the most gentlemanly way possible: no daggers or knocks on heads, just a quiet, orderly pestilence. I believe that only an English gentleman could see it this way, and we have no assurance that the angel was an English gentleman (though I'm not forgetting Pope Gregory's *non Angli sed angeli*). Such a one came a century after you, an English scientist. One day he demonstrated the synthesis of the elements of water in the presence of Queen Victoria, and he said: "The hydrogen and the oxygen will now have the honor of combining before Your Majesty!" My dear Sir, I trust you have learned by now that angels, hydrogen, and oxygen are in their own ways gentle —but their ways are not necessarily ours. Speaking as one of those vulgar Americans, I would say that the angel who did in those Assyrians sure smote 'em but good, whatever his technique. We read: "and when they arose early in the morning, behold, they were all dead corpses" (II Kings 19:35). Have you ever heard the case against arising early in the morning more neatly put?

To C. S. Lewis:

Mark Twain said that it wasn't the things in the Bible he didn't understand that gave him trouble—it was the things he did understand. I think that deserves a good label, like Twain's Law, according to which we cannot honestly plead ignorance of the Uncomfortable Words of God. You heartily agree, I'm sure. But you more than any other man taught me another truth, which does not contradict Twain's Law but complements it. Here is an example, from *The Problem of Pain*: "That we can die 'in' Adam and live 'in' Christ seems to me to imply that man, as he really is, differs a good deal from man as our categories of thought and our three-dimensional imaginations represent him; that the separateness . . . which we discern between individuals is balanced, in absolute reality, by some kind of 'interanimation' of which we have no conception at all." [5] According to Twain's Law, the Bible is full of things we can understand only too well. According to Lewis's Law, the Bible is full of things we cannot understand but had better believe. You are both right. Truth does not depend for its existence upon our ability to grasp it. As Henry Adams said: "After all, man knows mighty little, and may some day learn enough of his own ignorance to fall down and pray."

To Jonathan Swift:

In your day you noted: "We have just enough religion to make us hate, not enough to make us love one another." We have less than that now. In place of a religion that makes us either love or hate one another, we now have tolerance. We didn't choose this as the more excellent way; it was thrust upon us by political and social necessity. You were living in Ireland, not England or America, when you made your observation, and it may still hold true in Ireland. One night in August, 1971, thirteen people were killed in "religious" rioting in Ulster. The Irish have at least enough religion to hate each other. We who feel superior to them actually have less. (You excepted the then living saints, of course, and I except the now living ones: we're talking about the rest of us.) Most Americans and Englishmen think they are better off with a religion so slight that it makes nobody hate; but some of us believe that we must rise from our negligible religion of tolerance to that religion which will make us love one another, and without going through that dreadful intermediate stage. I don't know how we can make the colossal jump; but with God all things are possible.

To Peter Abelard:

In a letter to Heloise after your cruel final separation, you exclaimed: "What great advantage would philosophy give us over other men, if by studying it we could learn to control our passions!" There have been few wider and deeper tragedies in history than the digression of philosophy from its proper business. "The proper study of mankind is man"— and man is heart, soul, passions, as well as mind. A few philosophers, like Epictetus, have had that sound idea of their calling, but they have been exceptional. Here are a few modern comments on philosophy as it has become: "Any two philosophers can tell each other all they know in two hours"—Oliver Wendell Holmes, Sr.; "PHILOSOPHY. n. A route of many roads leading from nowhere to nothing"— Ambrose Bierce; "For there was never yet philosopher that could endure the toothache patiently"—Leonato, in Shakespeare's *Much Ado About Nothing*. When philosophy begins to help us to endure toothaches and heartbreaks patiently, it begins to justify its existence; hardly otherwise. You spoke of how philosophy would give us great advantage over other men if our study of it enabled us to control our passions. Wouldn't it give us something even greater—advantage over ourselves?

To Dwight D. Eisenhower:

A man as judicious and responsible as you deserves to be quoted with utmost exactitude after he has left this world. I'm sorry that this has not been the fate of your warning, in your farewell address as President, against the danger of "unwarranted influence" upon government by the "military-industrial complex." Almost everybody misquotes you as condemning, not that "unwarranted influence" but the "military-industrial complex" itself, which, of course, is simply our national defense system. How anybody can imagine that you, of all people, would condemn our national defense is incomprehensible; but there it is. What you are said to have said could have been said only by some kook or America-hater. Several months ago *Time* magazine repeated this distortion and I wrote to protest, quoting your exact words. A *Time* staffer replied that I was quibbling. This is the kind of quibble one would perpetrate if he said that there is a difference between "organized religion" and "unwarranted influence by organized religion upon government." That I can still so quibble reassures me that I haven't yet lost all my buttons, but I am worried about millions of Americans who can seriously believe that you warned us against national defense. All that I can do I will do, and that is to say to anybody who will listen: "Please check Ike's actual words. You may find that he did not, after all, advocate national suicide."

To William Temple:

During the past several months I've been rereading some of your writings. How well you wear! I am an avid collector of Christian epigrams, of which there are not nearly enough, and among the best in my collection is this one of yours: "For the religious man to do wrong is to defy his King; for the Christian, it is to wound his Friend." I have torn up innumerable sermons, letters, editorials, and other expressions of myself along the way because I found myself saying something that failed to meet the test of Christian validity that is in your saying, and undoubtedly I ought to have torn up many more for the same reason. For you, God is none the less our King, and you do not ask us to choose between a King-God and a Friend-God. As I understand you, what you say is that if we do not accept Christ's word that our King is our Father and Friend we are not Christian believers. Your distinction between the religious man and the Christian is getting serious attention today among us, especially by those who study the testamentary words of Bonhoeffer from his prison cell. What you say in this epigram seems to sum up Bonhoeffer's primary premise.

To Ralph Waldo Emerson:

If you were writing today you would have a hard time getting published, unless you abandoned this principle expressed in your Journals: "I would have my book read as I have read my favorite books, not with explosion and astonishment, a marvel and a rocket, but a friendly and agreeable influence stealing like the scent of a flower, or the sight of a new landscape on a traveller. I neither wish to be hated and defied by such as I startle, nor to be kissed and hugged by the young whose thoughts I stimulate." An admirable principle; and because you practiced it so well I find you a most refreshing and satisfying author. But a writer of today who wants to be read cannot go about his job in that spirit. Everything has to be what we call exciting—the excitement consisting of those very things you didn't want to do to your readers. You were not against excitement, but what you had in mind was quiet intellectual and esthetic excitement—and good incitement. The present-day appetite is for noisy and sensational literary fare. But I dare to hope for a swing back toward your more civilized taste, my reasoning being that readers are souls, and souls cannot permanently subsist on blood, thunder, and bombast.

To Alfred North Whitehead:

I do my best to correct those people who insist upon denouncing your definition of religion as "solitariness" without seriously reading it, but they seem to swarm invincibly. They equate solitariness with selfishness and they never explain why. Last week a prominent preacher was quoted in a news story as having called your definition the worst one he knew. "Real religion isn't a me-und-Gott affair," he patiently explained. "It isn't solitary but social." I cannot believe that he has ever sat down and read what you said about this, in *Religion in the Making*. For my part, your definition is about the best one I know, and I welcome an excuse for repeating it: "Religion is what the individual does with his own solitariness. It runs through three stages, if it evolves to its final satisfaction. It is the transition from God the void to God the enemy, and from God the enemy to God the companion. Thus religion is solitariness; and if you are never solitary you are never religious." [6] *Amen!* Your hostile witnesses never bother to note that you are talking about religion, not about Christianity as such. Even so, I keep remembering One who, when they came to make him a king, went up into a mountain, himself, alone (John 6:15).

To William Cowper:

Your hymn "God moves in a mysterious way" is one of my favorites. I sing it to myself and quote it to others constantly. But one sentence bothers me, the one in which you say of God that "behind a frowning providence he hides a smiling face." I don't like the sort of person of whom it may be said: "Old George is gruff and rude, and his employees quake before him, but underneath he's an old softy with a heart of gold." To hell with old George. I can't abide him. No man has a right to conceal his goodness if he has any. God is better than the best of men, and he cannot hide a smiling face behind a frowning providence. Sometimes, when I'm having a bad time, I can't see God's smile, but it isn't his concealment, it's my blindness, that prevents the vision. And sometimes when I see his frown, I know it is his love that frowns as it beholds some betrayal of his love by me. But I don't believe that God and old George have anything in common; and your line implies that they have. Here I am, presuming to tell you something about God, with me in my small corner and you in your large one in the Nearer Presence. However, I'm complaining about something you said when you were still in the flesh. I think you were wrong then. I think I am right about this particular matter now. I'm sure you are right about everything now.

To Sir Henry Maine:

With one of your respectfully remembered dicta, I must respectfully take issue. "War appears to be as old as mankind," you wrote, "but peace is a modern invention." We have no argument about the first part of your statement. Will and Ariel Durant, writing in 1968, report: "In the last 3,421 years of recorded history only 268 have seen no war." [7] But what on earth gave you the idea that peace has been invented recently, or at all? The belief that one has invented universal peace is no new thing. Alexander of Macedon and Augustus Caesar in their days were firm in that belief. Of course they were wrong, but they were as close to the truth, as well as far from it, as any man, any empire, any international peace-keeping institution up to the present moment. Did you think that the Pax Britannica of your day was a just, durable, universal peace? Of course; every civilized Englishman did. It is with no pleasure that I remind you of your error. Peace is still waiting to be invented. I think we have a better chance of inventing it if we keep clearly in mind that we haven't done so yet.

To Baruch Spinoza:

You were scornful of those who, when they theorize about the ultimate causes of things, "fly to the will of God," which, you say, is "the refuge for ignorance." If ignorance merits scorn, we are all hopelessly contemptible. No man can be always right; no man can know everything; no man can be entirely sure that he knows anything. If people "fly to the will of God" only to escape hard thinking, or unwelcome truths, they deserve your reprehension. But if what's in question is the ultimate causes of things or the ultimate issues of life— whence we came, why we are here, who and what we are, whither we go, a man may refer it all to the will of God saying "God knows; I don't. All I know is that God wills it." I feel no need to apologize to you or to anybody for believing that things exist and events happen because God wills them. I have read you searching for a better explanation, and I found none. I say this not ungratefully or unmindfully of all that you do for any fellow truth-seeker who sits down with you and looks at reality through the lenses of your wisdom and your sublime spirit of truthfulness in the quest of truth. I want to say only that, for some of us, belief in the will of God is not a *pons asinorum* but a step into the light. That step taken, we begin to see—or honestly believe that we do.

To Herman Melville:

You evidently took phrenology seriously in your day; but then every age has its superstitions, and some people take psychology seriously today. I infer from some words you put on the lips of Ishmael in *Moby Dick* that you took spinology even more seriously: "Now, I consider that the phrenologists have omitted an important thing in not pushing their investigations from the cerebellum through the spinal canal. For I believe that much of a man's character will be found betokened by his backbone. I would rather feel your spine than your skull, whoever you are. A thin joist of a spine never yet upheld a full and noble soul." Words fitly spoken! We Episcopalians have a family joke about a man being consecrated a bishop. In the solemn moment when the already-bishops were laying hands on him, his little son whispered, in awed tones: "Mummy, what are they doing to Daddy?" "Shhh!" she replied. "They're removing his spine!" A poor and disrespectful joke, I suppose; but if one were to rummage around in the long history of episcopacy, he might find an actual verifiable case, or even two, of a man who had a spine before his elevation to the purple but lacked one thereafter—explain it how you will. Well, there go some episcopal friends. While on the subject of spines, I might as well alienate some chiropractic friends as well. "It's going to rain," said the chiropractor to his patient. "I can feel it in your bones!"

To George Eliot:

There is something about the subject of marriage that makes it impossible for most discussants to say anything in a few words. It invites, almost demands extreme prolixity. But in one sentence, in Chapter 48 of *Romola*, you wrap up the whole question of motivation in marriage when you say: "Marriage must be a relation either of sympathy or of conquest." I am a clergyman of a church which requires me to sit down with every couple at whose wedding I am to officiate. On these occasions I often make your statement one of my texts. Of course, everybody agrees that marriage ought to be a relation of sympathy rather than of conquest, but such is the self-deception of our tainted nature that we (whichever our sex) sincerely believe that we are motivated by "sympathy" when what we are aiming at is "conquest." Some of us are never more aggressive in our real intentions toward somebody than when we imagine that our purpose is purely sympathetic and loving. Our "sympathy" can be the very weapon of our conquest; we love somebody in the way that the hospitable spider loved the fly. But of course you were keenly aware of this, and it in no way contradicts your statement. Marriage is indeed a relation either of sympathy or of conquest. It is good to have the options so clearly spelled out.

To James Boswell:

I cannot dote upon your learned, pious, but pompous friend at every turn of the way through your *Life of Johnson*. For example, I can only be disgusted by his comment upon the shooting affair between the Earl of Eglintoune and a poor commoner: "A poor man has no honour." This, from a Christian and a poor man himself, is contemptible. But soon after in your narrative he redeems himself. Discussing with you the possibility of eternal punishment he put forth the view that utterly unrepentant and reprobate souls may have to be eternally punished "to preserve in a state of rectitude both men and angels" who have this spectacle continually before them. As he spoke, however, his tone was such that you recorded: "He talked to me upon this awful and delicate question in a gentle tone, and as if afraid to be decisive." When Dr. Samuel Johnson was "afraid to be decisive" there was something unusual going on inside him! In this case, I doubt not it was the very grace of God. A Christian may properly speak of eternal punishment as a dreadful possibility for others and for himself; but unless he speaks of it gently, with awe, and with the pain of love, and "as if afraid to be decisive," he knows not what manner of spirit he is of; it is not the spirit of his Lord. A century before your time the learned John Hales grace-fully said: "Nobody would conclude another man to be damned if he did not wish him to be so." And that, of course, damns the damner.

To Bertrand Russell:

You were right about equality in America when you said: "In America everybody is of opinion that he has no social superiors, since all men are equal, but he does not admit that he has no social inferiors, for, from the time of Jefferson onward, the doctrine that all men are equal applies only upwards, not downwards." [8] There is some humbuggery in our equalitarianism. No American child, even, of normal mentality believes that John Dillinger and Abraham Lincoln were equals. But your countrymen can be pretty fuzzy about this, too. Many Englishmen reverently recall a remark the Duke of Wellington made at his wedding. The church was jammed with spectators so that the great man could find no clear path toward the altar. When a bobby tried to remove a shabby old woman from the line of march the Duke forbade him, saying grandly, "We are all equals—here!" The funny thing is that some people see nothing funny about this. We Americans have some praiseworthy ideals which are expressed in equalitarian terms: equality before the law, for example. At our best, we strive for them, and we all understand what "equality" means in such connections. But we need a more precise and restrictive word for it.

To Reinhold Niebuhr:

This morning I've spent some time testing with cases from history your statement: "Not much evil is done by evil people. Most of the evil is done by good people, who do not know they are not good." [9] When I came to Caiaphas I was convinced of the soundness of your maxim. It was not a man evil in himself who said: "Sometimes one man must die so that a whole nation need not die" (John 11:50). His principle was the greatest good of the greatest number, a morally very respectable principle. Well did Blake say of him:

> Caiaphas was in his own mind
> A benefactor of mankind,
> And read the Bible day and night.

And there is Hitler. He clearly believed that his mission was to regenerate the human race. He came not to destroy but to save. In that tortured soul we see a good man who did not know he was not good. It was this self-delusion that made him so monstrous a worker of iniquity. And St. Paul, by contrast, was an evil man, but he knew it and that is what makes the difference between a Paul and a Nero (another good man, who wanted culture for the masses). Paul knew that of sinners he was chief, that there was no health in him. By the grace of God this evil man did no end of good. Your paradoxical dictum seems to be unexceptionally true.

To Gilbert Keith Chesterton:

"I believe in getting into hot water," you once said. "I think it keeps you clean." You will like what an American Christian historian, Matthew Spinka, has since said along the same line: "Christians are the salt of the earth, and where else would one find salt but in the soup?" American Christians, like all others, have no strong natural taste for getting into hot water and soup; but with our famed national efficiency, we have perfected the ancient art of organizing ourselves away from the action. We get rid of many a hot potato by referring it to committee for further study. But one Episcopal bishop, the late Irving Peake Johnson, once said something very tactless about this practice. Fortunately for our peace of mind he was a wit, and so we can laugh it off. He said: "God so loved the world that he did not send a committee." You wonder how anybody like that ever got to be a bishop.

To Oscar Wilde:

You were the darling of the cultural rebels of your era, and that makes especially interesting and impressive this statement in *De Profundis*: "He who is in a state of rebellion cannot receive grace, to use a phrase of which the Church is so fond—so rightly fond, I dare say—for in life as in art the mood of rebellion closes up the channels of the soul, and shuts out the airs of heaven." Of course you were talking about rebellion against God and against Reality, a very different thing from the healthy and necessary rebellion one must wage against wrong things in himself and in the world. Somebody has well said that there is room for endless rebellion against ourselves. Perhaps we should call that the spirit of courageous self-correction. The rebel spirit you speak of is the Luciferian spirit, which slams the door in the face of God. It is the assertion of our vainglorious cock-of-the-dunghill ego against God's majesty and mercy. You spoke of it in the mood of that repentance which leads to life. In Aeschylean phrase, you had learned wisdom by affliction schooled. You always spoke beautifully. This time you spoke also with grace and truth.

To Arthur James Balfour:

"It is unfortunate," you lamented, "considering that enthusiasm moves the world, that so few enthusiasts can be trusted to speak the truth." Can't we make a distinction between enthusiasts with their pious hyperboles and liars with their lies? An Ananias or an Iago is one thing; a Romeo on the subject of Juliet quite another. Speaking of Charles Dickens's exaggerated art, Chesterton well reminds us: "We are all exact and scientific on the subjects we do not care about. We all immediately detect exaggeration in an exposition of Mormonism or a patriotic speech from Paraguay. . . . But the moment we begin to believe a thing ourselves, that moment we begin easily to overstate it; and the moment our souls become serious, our words become a little wild." [10] There is only one person we can ardently love and yet speak of without exaggeration: God. Because his perfections are infinite, they cannot be overstated. Speaking of anybody or anything else we love, we must stammer superlatives and occasional sublime inaccuracies. But we do not lie. When Romeo declared, "It is the east, and Juliet is the sun!" he was only trying to tell it as he saw it; and it wasn't a bad try for a young fellow. Juliet *was* his sun. I propose this distinction: The liar tries to direct us from the truth. The enthusiast tries to direct us to the truth, as he sees it. No words are adequate to his vision. That's why they sometimes, as GKC puts it, "become a little wild."

To Robert Frost:

I'm not a native of New Hampshire, nor have I ever lived there, nor do I intend to enter the N.H. primaries, but I execrate Emerson's saying: "The God who made New Hampshire taunted the lofty land with little men." Your fine poem "New Hampshire" is a literary honorable amend, but even you betray a kind of euphoric blindness when you say about New Hampshire people and other typical Americans:

> For art's sake one could almost wish them worse
> Rather than better. How are we to write
> The Russian novel in America
> As long as life goes on so unterribly?
> There is the pinch from which our only outcry
> In literature to date is heard to come.
> We get what little misery we can
> Out of not having cause for misery.
> It makes the guild of novel writers sick
> To be expected to be Dostoievskis
> On nothing worse than too much luck or comfort.[11]

The trouble with your guild of novel writers was not the lack of Russian-scale misery in the world around them, but the lack of Dostoievskian empathy within them. Theodore Dreiser lived in this unterrible land of too much luck and comfort, but he found all the raw material he needed for *An American Tragedy*. He didn't sit around the guild club deploring the absence of woe from his human environment; he got around among his neighbors with eyes, mind, and heart open. Even in New Hampshire I imagine that a novelist of such openness might find enough of the Tears of Things to agonize his art sufficiently.

To Wendell Phillips:

It was a few years before the Civil War that you told an audience: "Revolutions are not made; they come. A revolution is as natural a growth as an oak. It comes out of the past. Its foundations are laid far back." This was a wise word on a subject about which we hear much foolish talk. Americans generally like to think they are virtuosos at making good revolutions. They imagine that they have brought off several good ones in the past, and they have not. As you said, revolutions are not made, they come; and they do not come at our command or specifications. I find the sound theory of revolution in the Psalter: "God is the Judge; he putteth down one, and setteth up another. For in the hand of the Lord there is a cup, and the wine is red; it is full mixt, and he poureth out of the same" (Psalm 75:8-9). What we need is to see God's revolutions coming and then to get with them. Many of us don't like the idea that they are his, not ours, so we try to make our own. The result is always either a dud that doesn't come off or a horrible bloodbath that creates more problems than it solves. A true revolution is a work of God, aimed at reshaping the world after the likeness of the face of Christ. God does the mixing and pouring, but we can help, in our modest little way, by doing two things: keeping out of God's way, and doing the things he gives us to do as his "hands."

To Pierre Teilhard de Chardin, S.J.:

As you well know, modern Christians shy away from their own doctrine of Christ's Last Coming. Our biggest difficulty, I think, is one of conception rather than credibility, and here I find your statement wonderfully helpful: "When Christ appears in the clouds he will simply be manifesting a metamorphosis that has been slowly accomplished under his influence in the heart of the mass of mankind. In order to hasten his coming let us therefore concentrate upon a better understanding of the process by which the Holy Presence is born and grows within us." [12] You are commonly accused of teaching a concept of automatic evolutionary progress toward Christ as the Omega, but I think you amply stress the truth that man grows toward Christ only as he reaches and strives. In your call to such Christ-ward action, you affirm that the Christ who will appear is the Christ who is now preparing the hearts of his chosen (choosing) ones for that glorious reunion and reintegration with him. I hear in your words the cry of the first Christians: "Come, Lord Jesus!" Is there any more essential Christian prayer and longing than that?

To Edwin Markham:

Because you died less than 50 but more than 10 years ago your poetry must go almost universally unread, unhonored, and unquoted for some time yet. But I like to tell my Christian contemporaries that the radical theology of God-down-here which they find in Dietrich Bonhoeffer and Pierre Teilhard de Chardin is all there in your little poem *The Nail-Torn God*, well antedating those two great seers. In your vision there is "no God omnipotent,/ Seated serenely in the firmament,/ And looking down on men as on a host/ Of grasshoppers blown on a windy coast/ . . . But there is a God who struggles with the All,/ And sounds across the world his danger call:/ He is the builder of roads, the breaker of bars,/ The One forever hurling back the Curse—/ The nail-torn Christus pressing toward the stars,/ The Hero of the battling universe." Some might find this a bit florid and declamatory to their taste, but I love your rolling thunder. However, as a poet you are out, for the time being— awaiting what might be one day a glorious resurrection upon earth; but as a theologian you are already in—if only you were being read! I suppose it's easy to be patient under the conditions of eternity. Wait for another 50 years or so and somebody will rediscover you and launch you upon your posthumous career, and doctoral dissertations about you will blossom from sea to shining sea.

To Oliver Wendell Holmes:

On Julia Ward Howe's seventieth birthday you paid her this tribute: "To be seventy years young is sometimes more cheerful and hopeful than to be forty years old." It seems to me that she deserved a more intelligent tribute from a person of your intelligence. You ascribed her cheerfulness and hopefulness to a youth which she didn't have and didn't pretend to have. She was not one of those boring and pretentious people who try to be younger than their years. Their perfect description is written in Ecclesiastes 7:6: "For as the crackling of thorns under a pot, so is the laughter of a fool: this also is vanity." To be younger than one's years is always a form of infantile regression. I can't believe that you really preferred the company of such regressors to that of mature people, but I suspect that you were a victim of the superstition of which one of Oscar Wilde's characters says: "The youth of America is their oldest tradition. It has been going on now for three hundred years." You knew Mrs. Howe personally as I do not, but we all know what makes people like her radiant and joyful at seventy, or at thirty, or at ninety: their growing in grace as they grow in age. A person would have to grow *backward* to be "seventy years young." I'm very sorry you said it, for you were very wise, very good—and, alas, very quotable.

To Dr. Victor Heiser:

Well, you have died at last—at age 99, which says something about your theories of diet and health. Your long,
selfless, and fruitful crusade all over the world for public
health has blest countless millions of people; and I am sure
that somehow you still carry on your holy war against the
forces that destroy life. When you were orphaned at 16 you
learned your "first lesson in adult life—that nobody wanted
to be bothered with the problems of others." Instead of letting that turn you into a cynic and an opportunist, as do
those who embrace the philosophy of every-man-for-himself,
you chose to become the kind of person who makes the
problems of others his business: in your case, their problems
of pain, sickness, and preventable death. Of course we all
saw you as a diet faddist as well as a great healer, and I feel
that I must come clean about my response to some of your
prescriptions, which has been non-response. I knowingly risk
death before 99 by not restricting my breakfast to two
glasses of hot water. And the thought of alfalfa salad does
not "send" me at all; whatever the risk of abstinence, I ab-
stain. One precept of yours, however, I heartily embrace and
meekly obey: "Don't lose more than two pounds a week.
Give your skin time to pick up the slack." Right on!

To Confucius:

Any translation from your world and idiom to ours must be a colossal leap, and the English text of one of your aphorisms may be very wrong. It reads: "It is man that makes truth great, not truth that makes man great." If this is what you said, I must with all due deference take issue. A man once said to the universe, "I exist!" The universe replied: "So you do. However, the fact does not create in me any sense of obligation." Truth, like the universe, does not have to wait for any or all of us to come along to make it great. The earth was no less majestically globular throughout all those ages when everybody "knew better." Isn't the truth rather this? Truth shines forth in all its glory, for us to behold, when some soul consecrated to it embraces it, serves it, lives it. He's not making truth great; he's letting truth make him great. There is One who has done this for us so completely that he could even say, "I am the truth." I have a strong feeling that you would agree, if only we could get together and talk this over in a common language. Perhaps we shall one day.

To Francis Bacon:

I'm no busybody, of course, but I think you are entitled to know about an outrage against your dignity, if you don't already. You will remember your "charge concerning duells" in 1614, after a barber-surgeon and a butcher had presumed to engage in that sport of gentlemen. You impressively moralized: "I should think (my Lords) that men of birth and quality will leaue the practice, when it begins to bee vilified and come so lowe as to Barber-surgeons and Butchers and such base mechanical persons." I should think so, too. After that, duelling is for the guttersnipes, not for the carriage trade. But some years later, after your unfortunate impeachment and disgrace, some lewd fellow of the baser sort got to your noble essay and scribbled on the margin: "But you was afterwards put out for bribery." His ilk is still with us, making the lot of the moral policeman not a happy one: nasty snoops, with their damned *tu quoques!* Can't you imagine how His Majesty David the King detested that Nathan fellow? (II Samuel 12:1 ff.) If it weren't for them, being a professional moralist would be high and holy fun. I weep for you; I deeply sympathize. But (excuse me) when it happens to somebody else it's (ha! ha!) funny as hell (somebody else's).

To George Washington:

Nearly two hundred years ago you wrote in a letter to Henry Laurens: "It is a maxim founded on the universal experience of mankind that no nation is to be trusted farther than it is bound by its interest." If I didn't know the authorship of this statement and were asked to guess at it, I should answer "Edward Gibbon" instantly: it sounds like him. And it sounds cynical. That's why I would not think of you in connection with it. I doubt that a candidate for the American Presidency within the past thirty years could have said such a thing and been elected. But you were no cynical exponent of *Realpolitik*, and your statement turns out, upon careful analysis, to be not only correct as an observation but sound as a principle. A nation is never going to act beyond the limits of what it conceives to be its interest: that is observable and predictable fact. However, it can easily be wrong or shortsighted about what constitutes its interest. As I read your maxim, you say that no nation is to be trusted farther than it is bound by *what it conceives to be* its interest. A nation's conception of its interest: that is the crucial, decisive factor, always. It is the task of the statesman to see this true interest and to persuade his countrymen of it. This true interest may demand costly action on the other side of the planet, or even, in the world that is now coming into being, on other planets. But your maxim still holds true.

To Charles Dickens:

Probably the most universal of all critical platitudes is that your villains are so much more interesting than your heroes. Like most platitudes it is closer to truth than to falsehood. But for the record I think somebody should put in a word for the vivid power of some of your virtuous characters. Lucretius called this, in a man whom he revered, *vivida vis animi*. I see it shining in your Miss La Creevy (*Nicholas Nickleby*, chap. 38):

> "You never bestow one thought upon yourself, I believe," returned Kate, smiling.
>
> "Upon my word, my dear, when there are so many pleasanter things to think of, I should be a goose if I did," said Miss La Creevy.

It wasn't just talk. She obviously found pleasanter things to think of outside herself than inside herself, such was her *vivida vis animi*. Either she was a fool, or most of us have never got into the habit of thinking about others before thinking about ourselves and therefore cannot know what she's talking about. I suspect that she is not the fool, and in my very best moments I find such people far more interesting even than the Heeps, the Quilps, and the Ralph Nicklebys. Somebody who knew Elizabeth Barrett Browning found her endlessly fascinating, and explained: "'Twas her thinking of others made you think of her." As a Dickensian grateful for every crumb from your table, I wish you had spent more time with your Miss La Creevys, and less with your Dumb Dora Copperfields.

To Anonymous:

Some of us are too old and grouchy to be amused by your saying: "Religion often gets credit for curing rascals when old age is the real medicine." I wonder if you are familiar with this sweetly solemn thought by James Ball Naylor (*ob.* 1945):

> King David and King Solomon
>   Led merry, merry lives,
> With many, many lady friends
>   And many, many wives;
> But when old age crept over them—
>   With many, many qualms,
> King Solomon wrote the Proverbs
>   And King David wrote the Psalms.

And why not? What's so shameful or ridiculous if they did? If a man lives long enough to fall into "the sere, the yellow leaf," he should have some sage counsel and godly wisdom to pass along to the rest of us. Bless old Solomon for gems like this: "He that passeth by, and meddleth with strife belonging not to him, is like one that taketh a dog by the ears" (Proverbs 26:17). Or this: "Bread of deceit is sweet to a man; but afterwards his mouth shall be filled with gravel" (Proverbs 20:17). And bless the old Sweet Singer of Israel for such songs for our night as Psalm 103. Maybe it's old age that cures rascals, as you say; but then, God manages our ages too. At the very least it can be said for Solomon and David that they acted their ages at all their ages. I am deeply persuaded that few things please God more than that, in anybody.

To Ambrose Bierce:

When, in *The Devil's Dictionary*, you defined a saint as "a dead sinner revised and edited" you were a lot closer to a very orthodox Christian definition than you imagined. A parson could use your definition in instructing children in Sunday School. But of course you and he would mean different things by the same words. By a "dead" sinner you mean one who has physically died. But beginning with St. Paul and down to the present moment Christians have commonly spoken of being "dead" in sin and then being made "alive" in Christ. You would agree, I'm sure, that such an understanding of "death" as Kipling expresses in these lines in *The Old Men* is quite legitimate English:

And because we know we have breath in our mouth
    and think we have thoughts in our head,
We shall assume that we are alive, whereas we are
    really dead.

A saint begins to be a saint when he realizes that he is dead in his egocentricity and longs to come alive. He must be "revised and edited" by that Power not of himself that makes for righteousness. You think of the revising and editing done by piously mendacious hagiographers who, after the subject is safely dead, touch up and blow up the truth into a holy whopper. That this can happen is incontestable. But the revising and editing of the real saint is done by God, so that in the end the saint turns out to be just what you said —but did not mean: "a dead sinner revised and edited." Thanks for the good sharp definition. I can use it.

To C. S. Lewis:

I wonder about one thing you say in a passing remark in a letter to Malcolm. You wrote: "I think the 'low' church *milieu* that I grew up in did tend to be too cozily at ease in Zion. My grandfather, I'm told, used to say that he 'looked forward to having some very interesting conversations with St. Paul when he got to heaven.' Two clerical gentlemen talking at ease in a club! It never seemed to cross his mind that an encounter with St. Paul might be rather an overwhelming experience even for an Evangelical clergyman of good family." [13] Well, should it have crossed his mind? That's my question. Socrates never seems to me more truly a "Christian before Christ," an *anima naturaliter Christiana*, than when, in that heartbreakingly beautiful ending of the *Apology*, he expresses his hope for the life to come: "What would not a man give, O judges, to be able to examine the leader of the great Trojan expedition; or Odysseus or Sisyphus, or numberless others, men and women too! What infinite delight would there be in conversing with them! Surely, there they do not put a man to death for asking questions!" I have a deep feeling that you, and Socrates, and St. Paul, and your grandfather may have talked this over since you joined the company of heaven and that you have not found it such an "overwhelming experience" after all. Of course, if I'm wrong about this *I* may well be in for an overwhelming experience of reeducation on the point.

Author's References

1. *The Living Church*, December 20, 1970.
2. John Dewey, *Human Nature and Conduct* (New York: Modern Library, Inc., 1930), p. 5.
3. C. S. Lewis, *Beyond Personality* (New York: The Macmillan Company, 1944), p. 67.
4. Henry McKeating, *Amos, Hosea, Micah* (New York: Cambridge University Press, 1971), p. 27.
5. C. S. Lewis, *The Problem of Pain* (New York: The Macmillan Company, 1944), p. 74.
6. Alfred N. Whitehead, *Religion in the Making* (New York: World Publishing Company, n. d.), p. 16.
7. Will and Ariel Durant, *The Lessons of History* (New York: Simon & Schuster, Inc., 1968), p. 81.
8. Bertrand Russell, *Unpopular Essays* (New York: Simon & Schuster, Inc., 1951), p. 159.
9. Reinhold Niebuhr, *Essays in Applied Christianity* (New York: Meridian Books, n. d.), p. 136.
10. G. K. Chesterton, *Charles Dickens* (New York: Schocken Books, Inc., 1965), p. 18.
11. Robert Frost, *Poems* (New York: Modern Library, Inc., 1946).
12. Pierre Teilhard de Chardin, *The Divine Milieu* (New York: Harper & Row, 1960), p. 107.
13. C. S. Lewis, *Letters to Malcolm: Chiefly on Prayer* (New York: Harcourt, Brace & World, 1964), p. 13.